DISPOSABLE

DISPOSABLE

WHEN DATING IS NOT LOVING YOUR NEIGHBOR

DANIEL E. JOHNSON

FaithReasonCulture Press

Published by FaithReasonCulture Press
www.dangoodbooks.com

Cover concept: Daniel and Iris Johnson
Cover layout: Jenkins Graphics, East Orange, NJ

ISBN 978-1-7325084-0-8 (softcover)
ISBN 978-1-7325084-1-5 (e-book)

Printed in the United States of America unless otherwise indicated

CONTENTS

PREFACE

THERE IS A jungle out there in the dating world, and few that go there are unscathed. This book is not about how to navigate that jungle, nor is it about how to get something out of a relationship. Rather, the focus is understanding how the dominant dating culture operates and how it came to be, contrasting its dealings with what it means to love God and our neighbor, and encouraging everyone to embrace friendship—rather than selfishness—as the better basis for relationships, including romantic ones. This book conveys a message that likely anyone—Christian or not—who has concerns about the dominant dating culture can appreciate.

To at least some extent my views have been informed by my own experiences. In high school and even in college, I was ill at ease with the subject of dating and loath to participate. Like many, if not most, I felt like an outsider. I didn't like what I saw—especially the way people treated each other—and so I could never get comfortable with that culture. After becoming a Christian in college, my concerns were only heightened as I contrasted certain norms in the dating world with the behavior that God expects from us. In college I was fortunate—even privileged—to associate with groups of Christians who recognized the importance of friendship to both same-gender and inter-gender relationships. They lived their lives accordingly, and their behavior became an inspiration to me.

After college I continued to think about the dominant dating culture, read what others had to say, and engage in discussions with both men and women, in an effort to understand it from different perspectives—religious, cultural, historical, and psychological, all of which are reflected in this book. Now many years later, my concerns about that culture haven't changed much, nor has the way people treat each other, as it turns out. An older reviewer (my mother!) told me candidly that she wished she had known the things written in this book when she was dating. A younger reviewer told me: "This is not the book I would want to read, but it's the book I need to read."

I have written this book in the hope that the reader may be spared the agony that typically befalls those caught up in the dominant dating culture and instead find something much better.

Daniel E. Johnson

DISPOSABLE

PART ONE

The Heart of the Matter

Selfishness vs. Love

1

Dating and the Not-So-Trivial Pursuit of Desire

And they lived happily ever after.

*O*F COURSE, THEY didn't live forever, and they weren't always happy, but we're not told that part of the story because it's not as much fun. We are invited to believe, even at an early age, that a good marriage is problem-free, and high expectations of dating and romance are not far behind. Many think that developing a good relationship should be easy, that something should just "click" and then everything will be wonderful. Even the very nature of romance, especially when it is first kindled, is optimistic and positive. It is easy to imagine that there is an unbreakable bond of feelings that will always hold the two of us together! Over time, however, we become wiser and learn that this mindset is based on an exalted, unrealistic view of relationships. Our childhood views eventually give way to sober, perhaps even cynical ones, when we discover how relationships play out in the real world. Why so many relationships result in frustration and turn out badly, however, may not be clear.

What attitudes underlie dating? Everyone is different and brings his or her own beliefs and values to a dating relationship. Then there are different reasons for dating, such as a desire to find a boyfriend or girlfriend, wanting to spend time with someone, and looking towards getting married. So let's begin by taking a candid look at the *dominant* dating culture, especially as it is often practiced by many in the secular world. In so doing, it is necessary to make generalizations about people's behavior. Even if we have not personally experienced the dominant dating culture, we are probably familiar with it through the popular media or the experiences of friends.[1]

He Acts like This, and She Acts like That

For most men, physical appearance is the most important consideration in looking for a girlfriend. The typical man will first be attracted to, and then intrigued by, a woman's appearance. How he perceives her personality will also play a role in his thinking, but even his perception of her personality may be clouded by what he thinks of her looks. Not infrequently, he will imagine that a woman is a nice person simply because she is nice-looking, and he may even form a well-developed but unrealistic view of a woman before he really knows her.

The man is often the one to start the dating game, for example, by making phone calls or sending messages, which might be followed by one or more dates. Sex is an important goal of many if not most men, especially those who like to think of themselves as young and vigorous. So for them, dating is a means to this end, even though this is generally not stated explicitly. Some men may pretend to be caring and affectionate in the hope of getting sex in return, and others may be crude about it and pressure a woman to give into their demands. It's not that they are devoid of any desire for companionship or higher aspirations, but that is not what is foremost in their mind.

Men are perhaps easier to stereotype than women, because they are more likely to be driven by sexual urges and thus tend to be more one-dimensional in their thinking. Women are less likely to be driven by base instincts, and so it might be tempting to think of them as good and men as bad. This won't do, however: When we speak of *human* nature, we implicitly acknowledge that both men and women are imperfect and capable of doing bad things, that neither gender has a monopoly on vice.

A woman is more likely to approach the dating game wanting to have an emotional or psychological need met. She may want a man to make her feel wanted or important. A woman may find a guy cute or be attracted to some aspect of his personality, but at the same time she might be less interested in him as a person than in being entertained, enjoying the feelings that come from being desired, or finding satisfaction in having a relationship. A woman may long for romance, but if she idolizes it, she may want a boyfriend so that she can feel good later about her conquest—to feel a sense of empowerment that comes from the thrill of the chase. Some may even derive a perverse sense of satisfaction that comes from manipulating men, as when they "play hard to get." The crassest stereotype concerning men, women, and romance is that it is all about money in exchange for sex, a notion that is reinforced whenever the rich and beautiful agree to a prenuptial agreement, in which terms of divorce are agreed to prior to the marriage.

Since men and women are on different psychological wavelengths, they often perceive a relationship differently. In particular, men are inclined to measure progress in a relationship by how much physical activity is taking place, whereas women are more attuned to emotional bonding. Because we are all sexual beings, however, both men and women are conscious of the extent to which physical involvement is part of their relationships. Men have a tendency to push the envelope in what they can get away with. The last date's stopping point for physical involvement is assumed to be the minimum they can get away with next time. (In this way, one's conscience can be damaged incrementally.) Women who would otherwise object may be tempted to go along with this game, especially if they have a poor self-image. Thus, much of what transpires in the dating world stems from men's sex drive and the fact that some women are agreeable partners and others are willing to lower their standards to (temporarily) avoid being lonely.

Accordingly, many view increasing physical involvement over time as normal: On the first or second date, the man is permitted a low-key physical advance; on subsequent dates, a more aggressive physical advance is permitted, and so on, until at some point the parties engage in sex. This mechanistic progression is for many an unspoken rule that guides dating relationships, even though reducing a relationship to this sort of timetable is degrading. Ironically, for many, if the physical involvement has moved beyond the point with which they are comfortable, they may find it easier to break off the relationship completely rather than try to build (or rebuild) it.

Either party in a relationship is capable of manipulating the other. Men often view women as sex objects and treat them as such, with sexual favors being the goal. ("Just go for it!") Women who act in a manipulative way are likely to use psychological means, with the goal often being to gain some measure of control. ("She knows how to get what she wants!") Now of course, no one would ever say to someone else: "Hey! Do you mind if I use you?" That would be too simplistic. Instead, one *pretends* to be loveable and the sort of person who only thinks about others. So the pretender engages in a sort of *sophisticated* selfishness. To the extent that this charade is believed, the other person becomes vulnerable and learns to trust the pretender. This usually turns out to be a mistake, since sooner or later it will become evident that the relationship is not based on friendship or love but rather on wishes and desires. Genuine love and friendship are in short supply as this plays out; rather, they are continually confused with sex and selfishness.

As this exploitation continues, and especially when the relationship ends, feelings of animosity or even hatred can develop, which can be directed not just at the exploiter but also at the other gender in general. As negative emotions take over, the desire for developing a meaningful relationship with someone of the other gender might be put on hold temporarily, as the wounded person takes time to sort things out. As a sexual being, however, the aggrieved party still has a latent desire to connect with someone of the other gender, and after a time most will try again. In the next relationship, however, love and friendship may play less of a role than they did in the previous one as a result of the negative emotions and cynicism that have built up. This can easily become a vicious circle, and the negatively affected parties could be described as "walking wounded."

The Selfish Society,
Where Everything Is Disposable

As men and women get older and mature a bit, the stereotypes just described tend to deviate more from reality. For example, when men become marriage-minded, they may be less inclined to view women simply as "sex objects" and more as "marriage objects," taking into consideration the qualities that are desirable in a wife, as well as the need for a stable, long-term relationship.[2] But at any age the basic orientation of someone entering into a dating relationship is usually reflected in the questions: "What's in it for me?" and "How can I get what I want?"

It is clear that dating, as it is commonly practiced, is closely associated with selfishness. People generally do not date for the purpose of putting someone else's interests first. On the contrary, for most people the goal throughout the dating process, beginning with the initial contact, is self-gratification, the gratification of ego or lusts. The emphasis is on the romantic and/or physical at the expense of genuine friendship and true spirituality. The dominant dating culture reflects neither virtue nor unconditional love, but rather it is predicated upon the manipulation of others along with a kind of phoniness, a pretending to be someone else. The goal of such behavior is to gratify some selfish impulse. In short, the focus is on getting, not giving, and any "love" is conditional. In any relationship characterized by selfishness, the interests of the other person are subordinated. And so it is that typical dating relationships, which supposedly begin with a desire for the well-being of another, often end in a way that disregards that person's interests.

Selfishness in the dominant dating culture most clearly manifests itself in the attitude that human relationships, and by implication people themselves, are *disposable.* Some people get tired of a relationship and simply walk away from it, leaving their former partner behind like a discarded item. Some use people for the purpose of emotional gratification, for example, leading someone on until he or she makes himself or herself emotionally vulnerable and then, after having made the conquest, dropping that relationship before moving onto the next pursuit. Sometimes those who are already spoken for play the game of indicating a romantic interest in someone else in the hope that it is reciprocated, just to bolster their ego. However, the person who leads others on (to prove to himself or herself that he or she is desirable) is using others, not loving them. Still others play the game of hedging their bets, by keeping their relationship with a girlfriend or boyfriend secret while another potential suitor is in the running, giving them time to decide which one to keep and which to dump. Another way in which people are disposed of occurs in physical gratification without commitment, as in sex outside of marriage. People who engage in these behaviors are more concerned with their own desires and comfort level than in putting others first. Unfortunately, even a healthy desire to love and be loved is easily corrupted by our fallen, human nature into schemes for manipulating and using other people. The result is always that someone gets hurt: Being discarded can leave us feeling down and out, even worthless, since so much of our self-esteem is based on what other people think of us.

Sometimes people get discarded almost as soon as the relationship begins. The typical date itself involves minimal commitment, with the parties agreeing to meet each other for a few hours. Sadly, some are of the view that keeping even a "little promise" like this is subject to a whim, such as canceling or just not showing up. Such an attitude reflects the mindset that people are disposable, that it's okay to just leave them behind.

There are expressions that describe these rather prevalent behaviors, such as "use them and lose them" and "love them and leave them." They amount to saying that people are not really people anymore but rather objects that have worth only to the extent they can be used, and when they are no longer useful, they are to be discarded. The attitude that people are disposable—that if they interfere with what I want or don't serve my needs at a particular moment, I am justified in discarding them—exalts the desires of self above the needs of others. We live in a society in which seemingly everything has become disposable—and where people have correspondingly short attention spans and tire of things easily.

The language we use to describe relationships, which reflects our underlying attitudes, proves that we are often inclined to use people and to view them as objects, as the following examples further illustrate. A romantic prospect may be described as a "good catch" and someone may be encouraged to "play the field," but no one wants to be thought of as something to be caught or played with. It is one thing to try out a car or a pair of shoes, but to "try out" a relationship with a person often involves viewing that person as a "relationship object" rather than as a human being. A woman may "give in" to her boyfriend's demands, but this is hardly a description of mutual love and acceptance.

It doesn't help matters that sexual stimuli are all around us and are used to sell practically everything. This undue emphasis on sex leads us to believe that sex is more important than it is and leaves some longing for a sexual fantasyland that does not and cannot exist. A subtle but even more destructive message, however, is that sex and romance can be separated from any underlying human relationship. One effect of this message is that discarding people becomes easier, and another is that sex itself is degraded. All of this in turn affects our attitudes towards relationships in general, including marriage.

The Social Totem Pole

In view of the selfishness that permeates the dominant dating culture, how does dating as a social institution manage to function at all? At least a partial answer to this question lies in the fact that, in the world of dating, human worth is a relative commodity. People are not viewed as having intrinsic worth; rather, their worth is related to things that are transitory, such as their looks, how popular they are, and their current financial situation. A person is valued not so much for what is on the "inside" but rather for what is on the "outside" and what he or she has to offer. Based largely on worldly, temporal values people construct, if you will, a *social totem pole*, in which some are ranked higher than others. Although the ranking itself may be somewhat subjective and the criteria behind it may not even be well defined or explicitly articulated, people nevertheless have a good idea of where they stand, without being told. Those near the bottom of the social totem pole are painfully aware of their position—and feel stuck there—while those at the top enjoy basking in their status.

A rule of dating, which is generally unspoken, is that you look for someone near your level on the social totem pole. For example, rich guys may date pretty girls, and social outcasts find other social outcasts, assuming they find any-one at all. People may be constantly wondering if they are close enough to someone else's position on the social to-tem pole to be considered "worthy" of a date ("Am I good enough for that person?") or alternatively if they should set their sights higher ("Can I do better?"). We tend to seek out those we perceive to be near our level on the so-cial totem pole: People too far below us are beneath our dignity, whereas people too far above us we dare not ap-proach because that would be presumptuous. Our posi-tion on the social totem pole represents our worth or value in the social marketplace, which operates as an exchange rather than to facilitate the gift of love. Consequently, peo-ple typically fall in love with someone they think matches their own "worth." (To a lesser extent, a similar principle governs platonic, same-gender relationships, when men associate with men of similar standing to form cliques, with women doing the same.)

Occasionally it happens that two people at different ends of the social totem pole link up with each other, but the fact that such an occurrence is considered noteworthy underscores the extent to which our thinking is guided by such rankings. The headline "King Marries Pauper!" is surprising—not because the king got married but rather because of who he married. In a sense, dating is a sort of popularity contest in which those who are considered inferior are pushed aside or left out.[3]

So what defines one's standing on the social totem pole? Simply put, it's what the other gender is looking for. In their study of university life titled *Educated in Romance: Women, Achievement, and College Culture,* Dorothy Holland and Margaret Eisenhart reported:

> Women proudly proclaimed that they were going out with men who were "popular" on campus, known as sports figures, residents of the "best" men's dorm, or "outstanding" in their fields of study. Women were also proud to have it known that they dated men with the correlates or signs of prestige and attractiveness, a lot of money or especially nice clothes, apartments, or cars.[4]

On the other hand, the women found themselves in "a world of romance in which their attractiveness to men counted most. The women were subjected to a 'sexual auction block.'"[5]

On the college campus, then, and no doubt on the high school campus and most everywhere else as well, a woman's standing on the social totem pole is determined largely by how attractive she is, because that is what men are looking for, at least initially—obviously personality plays an important role at some point—whereas a man's standing is less well defined. (In college I knew a man who always, as the first order of business, wanted to meet his date's mother. Was he just being a gentleman? No, as he explained it, "I want to know what she'll look like in 25 years." You have to at least give him credit for thinking ahead.)

What about later in life? The hard-drinking student may be able to pass off his drinking as acceptable or even cool when in school, but if he doesn't change his ways, he will become a middle-aged drunk who will probably not rank highly. Conversely, the socially challenged bookworm who never attracted much interest from women may find himself in demand once he becomes a high-income earner, and the average-looking but hardworking and dependable female student may get a second look from a man once he becomes marriage-minded. Thus, one's ranking is subject to change over time and depends on his or her current social group. Also, this ranking may vary somewhat from group to group, since different groups will likely weigh various popularity-related factors differently.

How we stack up on the social totem pole is also related to the law of supply and demand, as in any consumer-based market. For example, if you are a woman and there aren't that many other women around, you are automatically higher on the social totem pole and can afford to be choosier than you otherwise would be—the same goes for men.[6] This underscores the intrinsically competitive and even adversarial nature of the dating process. It is a competition *between* those of the same gender (e.g., two men) *for* the attention of someone of the other gender (e.g., a woman).

However, once we outcompete those of our own gender and land a relationship, we may well face the ongoing prospect of doing battle with that significant other.

How Important Is Love to Dating?

If a dating relationship is pursued for very long, the parties may well imagine that they have deep and abiding feelings for one another or even that they are "in love." Most dating relationships end short of marriage, however, and especially when just one of the parties decides it is time to break up, any friendship usually ends at that time as well, with the outcome frequently being animosity. Someone who breaks off a relationship does not necessarily give much thought to the feelings of the jilted party, who is often treated like a discarded item. Frequently, the one who terminates the relationship is just glad to have it over with and be rid of the other person. When a "loving" relationship becomes one characterized by indifference, anger, or even hatred, it may be that the relationship was not as loving to begin with as might have been supposed. How ironic that there can be a bitter end to a relationship between two people who, in the early goings, imagined they had special feelings for each other!

Consider too the serial nature of dating at its worst—when someone's "love" is redirected from one potential suitor to another, resulting in a chain of disappointment and hurt feelings as people are discarded along the way. Given the way that dating is commonly practiced, it is not surprising that marriage is often practiced in a similar fashion—one relationship ends and another begins, only to end too, in due course.

While it is not true that "all is fair in love and war," this adage does underscore the difficulty people have in bringing a sense of decency to romantic relationships. The nations of the world thought it necessary to be guided by the Geneva Conventions in the conduct of war, but where are the conventions that govern the pursuit of "love"? Should we not at least conduct matters of "love" in a civilized way?

All of this is more than a bit unsettling. Even when our actions are right and, outwardly, we are ladies and gentlemen, inside we are likely preoccupied, not with something we can give but rather with something we want: a significant other, a relationship, or a marriage partner. So we feel tension, because on the outside we are one thing, but on the inside we are something else. In effect, we are shopping around, looking at the "produce" and asking ourselves: "Does it measure up to what I want?" Little or no time is spent reflecting on the questions: "What can I offer my friends and the world?" and "How can I be a more loving person?"

Friends or Lovers?

Many believe that it is possible, and even preferable, to decouple romance from friendship and that romance is the better thing to pursue. And why not? Isn't romance all about that magic moment when love takes over and everything is wonderful?

Tellingly, male/female relationships are generally viewed as being either in the "lovers" category or in the "friends" category, suggesting that the two are somehow mutually exclusive. It's as if we had to settle for one or the other. Lovers all too frequently allow base instincts and attitudes to drive the relationship. Friends may feel a need to explain that they are *just* friends, as if friendship were something to apologize for. A relationship that includes both friendship and romance is not necessarily the first thing that comes to mind.

Consequently, the dynamics of a date can be confusing. It may not be easy to know whether a gesture is being made out of love or selfishness. For example, the man may offer to pay for the evening out. Does he do this because he is a naturally loving and generous person, or is he perhaps looking for something from his date in return? If the woman offers to help pay, is it because she wants to graciously share the financial burden or because she wants to ensure that he doesn't have a claim on her?

Since some pretend to be generous when they are actually selfish, even a sincere expression of friendship can be easily misinterpreted as simply a desire to get something in return. It's not always easy to read other people's intentions—for that matter, it may not even be easy to understand our own intentions—all of which can lead to a certain tension in a relationship, particularly one that is just beginning. Confusion over roles and the tension that naturally flows from this seem to be integrally woven into the social fabric of the dating culture.

There is also a sense in which the dominant dating culture—apart from its manifest selfishness—actually makes it difficult to establish a friendship, for those who would want that. Because going out on a date is considered by most to be something of a big deal ("How did it go tonight? I want details!"), the stakes are high at the outset, and as a result the man (if he is the initiator) may be reluctant to ask and the woman may be reluctant to accept. If asked, the woman may think to herself, among other things: "He hardly even knows me. What is he up to?" The man, on the other hand, knowing full well that the woman probably thinks this way, has reason to shy away from asking, because he may have no assurance that she will accept if he does ask. To get the ball rolling, both persons must reach some level of (tentative) interest in the other before the dating process gets started. However, before two people really know each other, can any such interest be based on anything meaningful? So situations can arise in which one feels forced to make a premature evaluation of another person. Moreover, the act of asking for a date (or accepting a date) may either communicate greater interest in the other person than is really there or stem from more interest in the other person than is justified. Thus, to the extent that significance is attached to a date—as opposed to it being viewed as a casual event—it becomes difficult to make a date or to work towards establishing a friendship.

The Desire to Be Accepted, the Fear of Rejection, and Role Playing

We all want to be accepted for who we are, but we generally have doubts as to whether this is possible. At some point in our lives most of us have a poor self-image and may experience nagging feelings of despair, loneliness, rejection, isolation, worthlessness, and self-pity. For many, self-pity and the fear of rejection ("Other people think I'm no good and will never like me!") can be crippling and lead to unhealthy habits, such as constantly analyzing every social situation for signs of acceptance or rejection ("Where is this relationship at right now?"). We worry about our looks, fixate on what other people think of us, and become discouraged when we go six months without a date. The dating game is fraught with tremendous pressure to be accepted, to not be rejected, and to act in a certain way—it exacts a huge psychological toll on its participants.

It is easy to let what others think of us determine our self-image and to imagine that without a romantic relationship we are incomplete. After all, society is constantly telling us that the meaning of life is to be found in romance, sex, girlfriends, and boyfriends—and that a person's worth revolves around his or her sex appeal. The thought of being incomplete may gnaw away at us and urge us to chase someone—or anyone—which can leave us in a state of constant tension. If we become desperate and fixated on someone in particular, this puts us under still more pressure. ("I really do want that person. Is there any chance at all that it's mutual?") If we are unattached, we may fret over whether we will ever find a girlfriend or boyfriend. Some are tortured with such questions as: "How often should I date to be considered respectable?" and "How can I find my next date?"

The gap between what we want (a relationship) and what we might get if we are too forthcoming (rejection) tempts us to pass ourselves off as people other than who we really are. We are afraid that, if we show our true selves, we won't be liked, especially if we've been rejected previously for having done so. We are reluctant to be honest and transparent about who we are, since we are afraid that, if the truth about us comes out, any chance for a meaningful relationship might be doomed.

As a consequence, dating is typically carried out on a stage in which the participants pretend to be people other than their true selves, to impress the other person and out of fear that if the "real me" comes to light, rejection will follow. This fear of rejection, as well as the role playing that often accompanies it, can lead to ongoing anxiety. Sooner or later, of course, the real me will come to light and we will become known, just as we will eventually see through any masks that the other person is wearing. (Fewer couples would have been nervous on their first date had they known then what they subsequently learned about each other.)

The game of appearances is phoniness that is part of the dating culture. It guarantees that, as long as this game is played, the relationship will be superficial and fail to be as meaningful as it should be. It also ensures that we will still have doubts about our self-worth, since as long as we are not honestly disclosing ourselves, the real me has not been accepted. It stymies our personal growth, since we are pretending to be persons other than ourselves. Indeed, to the extent that the "fake me" is accepted, we are tempted to hide our true selves. We avoid being honest because we are insecure.

Couples who are especially immature may want to impress not just each other but any onlookers. They show off and want our applause. Such a show involves using the other person, by putting him or her on stage in a way that is designed to make the partner look good. Some in romantic relationships manifest their insecurity by conspicuously and consciously seeking the attention of others through public displays of affection. This amounts to treating a significant other as an object to be flaunted, in order to be temporarily noticed by whoever happens to be watching. This behavior has its roots in insecurity—a sense of inadequacy and a desire to be approved by others—and reflects the attitude that a significant other is a trophy, a possession, or a prize to be put on display.

Other Unhealthy Tendencies

Almost everyone has a desire to be connected with someone of the other gender, and most view some version of dating as the way to get there. Since the dominant culture would have us believe that we are incomplete without a boyfriend or girlfriend, it is easy to believe that we really should be married or at least dating someone! Some view themselves as outright failures if they are not a part of the dating scene. So we may feel a need to date, as if somehow our humanity depended on it. Henry David Thoreau observed that most people "lead lives of quiet desperation," but this must be doubly true when it comes to dating.[7] For some, their whole reason for living becomes wrapped up in finding or in keeping some significant other. Small wonder, then, that being jilted can lead to so much hurt.

In view of the enormous pressures to be attached to someone, those who are lonely are susceptible to "falling in love" with the first person who shows any interest in them: When only one potential boyfriend or girlfriend is around, our mental energies tend to focus on that person. We begin looking for ways to find romance, even if it is against our best judgment ("This may be my only chance!"), a tendency that is only reinforced by a bad self-image ("I won't ever find anyone else who will like me—I'm just not good enough"). Unfortunately, a bad self-image leads to bad judgment, which results in bad decisions.

A related tendency is to become infatuated with someone—here a person is viewed as something to be mentally manipulated rather than as someone to be loved. Infatuation is motivated by wishful thinking, the desire to see one's dream come true. So a rosy or even perfect view of someone is developed without good reason to back up the opinion. We want to believe the best of someone when we are in a dating relationship, even if objectively speaking there might not be a solid basis for that optimism, particularly in view of past experience. It can easily become a case of the "triumph of hope over experience."[8] Unfortunately, believing something about someone that is untrue can only lead to disappointment when the bubble of unjustified expectations bursts. Having romantic expectations of someone amounts to placing demands on that person, and such demands on another person will generally go unsatisfied. Sooner or later, after reality sets in, the person who has run down Fantasy Lane may even experience feelings of rejection (even if he or she was never actually rejected) and may even have difficulty relating to the person who was formerly the object of infatuation, because the idol that had been constructed is still lingering about in the recesses of the mind.

Because we crave love and attention and want so much to be successful in the dating realm, it is most unpleasant being turned down for a date—nor for that matter is one comfortable in turning another person down. In either case a feeling of weirdness is often the result, with the tendency being to avoid the other person until the encounter is forgotten or at least recedes into the back of the mind. Then there is the pain that goes along with being dumped after a relationship has been established. Unfortunately, it is in the nature of human psychology that one negative experience makes as much of an impression on us as several positive ones. In view of the great potential for negative experiences in the world of dating, those that thrive there tend to be either callous or thick-skinned. Sensitive people, who are unwilling to pay the often heavy psychological price of finding a significant other, are sometimes inclined to avoid the dating scene altogether.

How a Dating Relationship Might Progress

Dating, as it is often practiced, includes various phases. At the outset, a man will pursue a woman for whom he has a physical attraction, whereas a woman is more likely to be prompted by an emotional and/or psychological attraction. The man is likely to push the sexual limits as soon as possible and throughout the relationship. Character and values often play a minor role for both genders in the initial assessment, but they will probably become important later. ("He cheated on me!" "She turned out to be kind of weird!")

Perceptions of the other party are likely to change significantly over time, as reality sets in and displaces any image that one constructed of the other person along with any exhilaration that one initially experienced. Infatuation and getting to know someone well are mutually exclusive.

Herein lies a potential danger to a relationship that explains why many are prone to go off the rails: When another object of desire presents itself (e.g., another attractive person comes along), it may seem to be more inviting and desirable than what the current relationship has to offer. The grass is always greener somewhere else.

Things like common interests and goals are important to how a relationship progresses. In their absence, the relationship will likely fizzle out. Once some kind of romantic relationship has been established, months or years may be spent trying to force a square peg into a round hole until one or both parties give up trying. An initially superficial relationship must either die or give way to a more meaningful one based at least in part on common goals and interests, which the parties may or may not realize they share (or don't share) at the outset.

Although a relationship may lead to something permanent, it is more likely to continue for a while "till death do us part…or I find someone better," as a friend of mine used to put it sarcastically. Many who marry do so when they think they have probably found the best deal they can realistically hope for, given an assessment of what they have to offer—that is, they believe they have found an acceptable match on the social totem pole. At that point, they decide to make the best of it, even if that means tolerating each other for as long as they can.

Dating Culture Revisited

There is no single dating culture, and even the terms "date" and "dating" mean different things to different people. The stereotypes of dating and the roles that men and women play outlined here by no means describe all the behavior that goes on in the world of dating, but they do describe *a lot of it.* As such, they provide an important reference point that can help guide our thinking. These stereotypes are concerned with attitudes and behavior that are in the back of our minds when we approach the subject of dating—or perhaps even in the front of our minds. For this reason alone, they can't be ignored. A man and a woman who venture out on a date may not just be wondering if they are liked by the other person. Rather, the woman is very possibly on her guard, and likewise, the man may think to himself at some point: "What does she want from me?" So these stereotypes can lead to confusion, even if we do not embrace the values of the dominant dating culture, since we can't be sure what other people's attitudes are before we get to know them.

Essentially, the dominant dating culture offers us a consumer-based approach to relationships. We shop around for relationships in what has been called a "meet market," with one eye on what we want and the other on what we think we can realistically get: A "good match" between two people is thought to take place when their relative worth on the social totem pole matches and each one gets something desired. As with any consumer item, however, the relationship (and thus the person) is considered disposable. The setting for all of this is an environment in which friendship is devalued and selfishness is dominant. Accordingly, we are likely to approach the subject of dating with unease.

*   *   *

Do we look back on previous relationships with pride? Does romance live up to its promise? The retrospective view of romantic relationships is quite different than the forward-looking one. All too often, the optimism of "they lived happily ever after" gives way to cynicism, and hope gives way to regrets. We can't help but wonder: Isn't there a better way to form and nurture relationships?

Questions for Reflection and/or Discussion

Have you known people who were treated *badly* in a dating relationship? If so, what did they experience? How did it change them?

Have you known people who were treated *well* in a dating relationship? If so, what did they experience? How did it change them?

In a dating relationship, men and women often enter into a sort of exchange. What do men offer and what do they get in return?
What do women offer and what do they get in return?

Have you found people at the top of the social totem pole to be humble? How would you characterize the behavior of those at the bottom of the social totem pole?

Is there any aspect of the dominant dating culture that you like?
What if anything about dating bothers you the most?

How would you describe the state of affairs between the genders today?
To what extent do dating relationships contribute to that?

Imagine a world in which there was no true love at all—no unconditional love—and people were always selfish.

What would relationships between the genders be like? How different would those relationships be from what we have now?

Is the notion that "people are disposable" at the heart of other problems in our society besides the dominant dating culture? If so, which ones?

2

What's Love Got to Do with It?

And over all these virtues put on love, which binds them all together in perfect unity.

—Colossians 3:14

As DESCRIBED IN the preceding chapter, the all too common dating relationship involves selfishness masquerading as love: Someone pretends to offer love, while having something else in mind. Self-centered desires come first, and people are used instead of loved. In the end, everyone feels empty. Is this what God wants for us?

God's Good Creation...and What Went Wrong

This brokenness is not what God had in mind in the beginning, when He created the first human beings: "The LORD God said, 'It is not good for the man to be alone. I will make a helper suitable for him.'" (Genesis 2:18) Even before sin entered the world, when everything in the world was still perfect, it was not good to be alone. God makes it clear that we are meant to be with other people. A subsequent verse records Adam's reaction to Eve:

> "This is now bone of my bones
>   and flesh of my flesh;
> she shall be called 'woman,'
>   for she was taken out of man."
>
> GENESIS 2:23 (NIV)

Romance always invites us to believe the best. Adam's expression of love is no exception and suggests he had only the highest expectations for her and their relationship—and why not? Eve was perfect for him, having been created especially for him. It could even be called a "marriage made in heaven." Genesis makes it clear that we are sexual beings. The desire to be with and intimately know someone of the other gender, to love and be loved, is a God-given one. This desire has many facets, including a longing for togetherness, friendship, and a sense of belonging.

Things changed when sin entered the world. Even before God pronounced His judgment and curse, however, there was already confusion about what it means to be sexual beings. After eating the forbidden fruit

> the eyes of both of them were opened, and they realized they were naked; so they sewed fig leaves together and made coverings for themselves.
>
> Then the man and his wife heard the sound of the LORD God as he was walking in the garden in the cool of the day, and they hid from the LORD God among the trees

of the garden. But the LORD God called to the man, "Where are you?"

He answered, "I heard you in the garden, and I was afraid because I was naked; so I hid."

And he said, "Who told you that you were naked? Have you eaten from the tree that I commanded you not to eat from?"

GENESIS 3:7–11

Adam alludes to tension in his relationship with Eve when he responds to God by saying: "The woman you put here with me—she gave me some fruit from the tree, and I ate it." (Genesis 3:12) Evidently, the world's very first couple was no longer getting along so well and the loveless blame game was under way.

While Adam and Eve could have lived happily ever after, they made choices that prevented that from happening. They initially had perfect love for each other, but this perfection came to an end when sin entered the scene. Sadly, for many, relationships with the other gender have brought more pain than joy, but this is not the way things were meant to be.

God's Call to Love One Another

Men and women are attracted to each another because they are made that way—this is not an attraction that needs to be learned! What we do need to learn in our post-Eden world is how to channel our desires in a productive and wholesome way. In order to experience romantic love as it was intended to be—as *God* intended it to be—moving away from sin and towards God is a move in the right direction. Since God created sex, romance, and love, His advice to us is worth heeding. His prescription for all broken relationships in this fallen world can be summarized in the words "unconditional love."

God extends covenant love to us, and He expects us, in a like manner, to extend love to one another:

> "Teacher, which is the greatest commandment in the Law?"
>
> Jesus replied: "'Love the Lord your God with all your heart and with all your soul and with all your mind.' This is the first and greatest commandment. And the second is like it: 'Love your neighbor as yourself.' All the Law and the Prophets hang on these two commandments."
>
> MATTHEW 22:36–40

But does the commandment to "love your neighbor" apply to dating? Or would that be reading too much into this commandment? Jesus was once asked by an expert in the law: "And who is my neighbor?" (Luke 10:29b) Jesus responded with the Parable of the Good Samaritan, who was an unexpected friend to someone who had fallen victim to robbers. Tellingly, Luke records that the expert in the law asked Jesus this question in order to "justify himself" (Luke 10:29a). So it is with human nature. Left to our own devices, we avoid loving people unless it suits our purposes. Jesus, however, did not embrace a narrow understanding of the word "neighbor" but rather a broad one. In fact, he went so far as to say that we should love our enemies (Matthew 5:44, Luke 6:27)—how much more, then, should we love those we call our lovers! Regardless of whether we care to accept it, there is no exception to the Golden Rule when romance is involved.

Various passages in the New Testament explain in greater detail what it means to be a loving person. For example, 1 Corinthians 13 contains oft-quoted passages that speak directly to how we should view ourselves and treat others.

> Love is patient, love is kind. It does not envy, it does not boast, it is not proud. It does not dishonor others, it is not self-seeking, it is not easily angered, it keeps no record of wrongs. Love does not delight in evil but rejoices with the truth. It always protects, always trusts, always hopes, always perseveres.
>
> Love never fails.
>
> 1 Corinthians 13:4–8a

Although it is not easy to live up to these teachings, we instinctively recognize they are right, and we expect everyone else to treat us accordingly. When we don't treat others this way, however, a self-serving double standard is at work in us.

Love and Our Relationships with God and His People

The two great commandments God has given us are first to love God and second to love our neighbor as ourselves. So God is to be the center of our (love) life! Indeed, it is difficult to see how one can do well at the second commandment, while ignoring the first.

God wants us to have the best. Since He does care for us, we have a rational basis for loving Him, for trusting Him. He is worthy of our trust, and He wants us to trust Him so that we will have the best in life. Going it alone, without God, is hardly a formula for a successful love life. Jesus said: "But seek first his kingdom and his righteousness, and all these things will be given to you as well." (Matthew 6:33) Although Jesus here is specifically addressing food and shelter, it is nevertheless true that, as a general principle, when we pursue something to the exclusion of God, we won't end up happy or satisfied.

To have the best possible friendship with anyone (male or female), we need to be right with God. Jesus said, "I am the vine; you are the branches." (John 15:5a) We're not at the center of the universe, as much as we might want to believe it. Rather, our lives have meaning to the extent that they revolve around God. It is easy to forget this and believe that things of this life—like romance—will satisfy us at the deepest level, and God is just something that we are supposed "to do" when we get around to it or find the time. But Jesus teaches that the things of this life have their deepest meaning only when we are properly connected to God.

Blaise Pascal observed that within everyone resides a certain emptiness and that "this infinite void can only be filled by an infinite and immutable object, that is to say, only by God himself."[1] Unfortunately, we have a tendency to nurture within ourselves cravings for satisfaction, pleasure, and attention, among other things, none of which can ever fill up this "infinite void." This cult of self that drives these cravings chokes out love and allows anxiety to grip our hearts. If that is not bad enough, just as "perfect love drives out fear" (1 John 4:18a), fear has a tendency to drive out love—love of others, love of God, and the proper love of oneself.

Even though love emanates from God and loving God is the greatest commandment, love doesn't stop there. God expects us to live out our faith in the context of community, in relationships with other people. Within this faith community, this kingdom of love, we are brothers and sisters and share a certain kind of equality before God. This is not a place for rankings or trying to get ahead. Moreover, since living out our lives in the context of community is God's expectation for us, pursuing dating relationships to the exclusion of other relationships and friendships is neither Biblical nor healthy. Jesus said: "By this everyone will know that you are my disciples, if you love one another." (John 13:35) This is a challenge to those of us who call ourselves Christians: that people would know that we are different by the way we treat each other, including those we date.

What Does It Mean to Love as a Practical Matter?

Love involves concern for another person's well-being. It means encouraging that person to grow spiritually, emotionally, and intellectually, while maintaining a clear conscience and purity. We read in the book of Philippians:

> Do nothing out of selfish ambition or vain conceit. Rather, in humility value others above yourselves, not looking to

your own interests but each of you to the interests of the others.

In your relationships with one another, have the same mindset as Christ Jesus.

Philippians 2:3–5

Most of all, then, love for another means putting that person first, ahead of our own interests, without expecting something in return. John Powell offered this insight in his book *Unconditional Love*:

> There is no third possibility: love is either conditional or unconditional. Either I attach conditions to my love for you or I do not. To the extent that I do attach such conditions, I do not really love you. I am only offering an exchange, not a gift. And true love is and must always be a free gift.[2]

So love is not the giving of rewards to someone in exchange for something we want. Likewise, romance is not really love if it is not accompanied by true friendship, which is more than simply hanging out together—it involves warmth, caring, mutual respect, two-way communication, forgiveness when needed, and loyalty, among other things.[3] Indeed, the great commandment to love our neighbor must mean at the very least being a friend or it means nothing. Moreover, it is not true (even though many seem to think so) that being in a loving relationship is like being in a state of nirvana or that a loving relationship can run on autopilot. Generally, it will take work and even be hard at times.

Since Jesus commands us to love, we must decide whether to keep this commandment. It follows that love is based on a decision and involves the ongoing working out of commitment.

Unconditional Love vs. the "Love" of the Dominant Dating Culture

We do not live in a loving society but rather one in which the emphasis is on *me*, on self-satisfaction. The dating world is no exception. The dominant dating culture would go so far as to have us believe that people are disposable—that they are to be used and then discarded.[4] Some even believe that we are enriched by having as many sexual partners as possible and that we are to *get* something out of each one of them. The most that the dominant dating culture has to offer is that both parties in a dating relationship should feel good or be satisfied as they mutually exploit each other.

The selfishness of the dominant dating culture is clearly at odds with Jesus' teachings: "It is more blessed to give than to receive." (Acts 20:35b) The paradox of life and love is that by giving of ourselves, we receive. And yet we are tempted to abandon love and focus only on ourselves when dating. If the words of Jesus are true, however, there is no reason for us to believe that we will find happiness this way. We are to use things and love people—not the opposite!

"Love" in the dominant dating culture is conditional and is based on "merit"—that is, where one stands on the social totem pole. But this is not how God views us: Each of us is of great worth, because we are created in the image of God (Genesis 1:27) and we reflect His image even in our fallen state (2 Corinthians 3:18). Moreover, we are valuable enough to God that He had His Son die for us as part of His great redemption plan for humanity. These truths apply to each of us, regardless of looks, popularity, financial worth, social standing, and gender.

The contrast between the love of the dominant dating culture and the unconditional love called for in the Bible could not be starker. The one is self-centered, the other self-less. The one treats people as disposable, the other acknowledges that people have great worth (that they are worth saving, in fact) and are to be treated as neighbors. The one is preoccupied with immediate gratification ("Live for the moment!"), whereas the other is willing to make sacrifices, takes time, and is grounded in values that last. Imagine if God's love for us were like our "love" for each other: tentative, fickle, self-serving. Would there be a Good Friday and an Easter Sunday?

Which Kind of Love Really Works?

It is obvious which kind of love (unconditional love versus selfish "love") is more likely to lead to a long-lasting relationship. Indeed, it is difficult to see how dating, as it is commonly practiced, can lead to anything other than brokenness in the long run. Upon reflection, it is clear why this is the case.

A loving person is someone we are instinctively drawn to for the long term, because that person has our best interests at heart. On the other hand, someone who is only looking out for himself or herself is not someone we want to be around for very long. No one wants to be taken advantage of.

A loving person is one who can be trusted, since he or she has no hidden agenda and no desire to take advantage of or use another person. It is difficult to imagine how any relationship can grow in the absence of mutual trust. Without trust, two people will always doubt each other's level of commitment and be nagged by the question: "How much longer will this relationship last?"

A loving person is also a forgiving person. In any relationship between two fallible human beings, there is the potential for hurt feelings and damaged egos. This is especially true in a romantic relationship, in which expectations may be high and motives less than pure. How we choose to respond to hurt is critical: Nursing old wounds is a barrier to maintaining a healthy relationship and stifles its growth. On the other hand, a willingness to forgive makes a new start possible.

Is it reasonable to expect that a truly loving relationship can develop from one that is based on selfishness? While many things are *possible*, not everything is *probable*! A relationship that has its roots in selfishness does not have a good start and generally will lead to frustration, since true friendship and love may never materialize. It is small wonder, then, that many relationships (and even marriages!) begin and later end without the parties ever making friendship the center of their relationship. When we are motivated by selfishness, and when self-indulgence of any kind is the goal rather than cherishing and loving another person, the relationship with that person suffers and the participants are impoverished or emotionally shipwrecked. Sexualizing romance fosters a lack of respect for the other person, making friendship and genuine affection even more difficult. Selfishness is ultimately self-defeating.

A focus on oneself *promises* great rewards and fulfillment but ironically leaves one less fulfilled in the end. It has been said that sin promises so much but delivers so little. Selfishness doesn't lead to lasting satisfaction but rather to emptiness, and the longer it is practiced, the emptier, more broken, and less satisfied we become.

The Dominant Dating Culture vs. Christian Virtue

The Bible does not specifically address the practice of dating, which itself is a relatively recent phenomenon, but it does say many things that have a bearing on this subject. Consider, for example, the following four aspects of the dominant dating culture.

1. *The superficial way dates are chosen*

For men, looks are usually all-important; for women, it might be some aspect of a man's personality that captivates them. On the other hand, Solomon wrote: "Charm is deceptive, and beauty is fleeting; but a woman who fears the LORD is to be praised." (Proverbs 31:30) Two things that the Bible so strongly cautions against—charm and beauty—play a dominant role in the dating world. For men, beauty is what they notice and what they pursue. For women, charm is something they project when being a tease or a flirt, in order to get what they want. For that matter, how many men wouldn't enjoy the role of Prince Charming? Of course, our perception of people is subject to change, and if we decide that someone is no longer beautiful or charming, our desire (or lust, as the case may be) may find a new object of attention.

2. *Pretending to be someone else, other than the real me, in order to gain someone's favor (or to avoid rejection)*

Integrity, on the other hand, is a virtue, which Jesus praised: "When Jesus saw Nathanael approaching, he said of him, 'Here truly is an Israelite in whom there is no deceit.'" (John 1:47) At first glance, Nathanael may not seem like a role model for us when we think about dating. But perhaps we should ask ourselves: How did he engage women in his era, and how would he engage women today? Just to ask these questions gives us pause, as we are confronted by the difference between his character and our own. Imagine a world in which everyone was honest, all the time, and there was "no deceit" in anyone. Would such a world have more successful relationships or fewer?

It is self-defeating to play the game of pretending to be someone else and not reveal one's true self because of the fear of rejection. The dishonesty that pervades the dating culture leaves us wondering what the status of a relationship really is: "Does she *really* like me, or is she just pretending?" "Does he *really* love me, or is he just saying that to get something?"

3. *The time and effort spent on dating-related pursuits*

Consider the effort people make in looking for someone special versus the effort they devote to others or even the time they spend improving themselves. It is only fair to ask: Are we making the most of our time? Once again, Jesus said: "But seek first his kingdom and his righteousness, and all these things will be given to you as well." (Matthew 6:33) Consider also this sobering note from James: "What is your life? You are a mist that appears for a little while and then vanishes. Instead, you ought to say, 'If it is the Lord's will, we will live and do this or that.'" (James 4:14b–15)

4. *Infatuation, in which someone becomes a "perfect" object that is manipulated in the mind of another*

The manipulator becomes attached to an image rather than to the real person and in that sense exchanges truth for a lie, since no one is perfect: "for all have sinned and fall short of the glory of God." (Romans 3:23) Pop culture, including the lyrics of many songs, would have us believe that there is someone out there who is just right for us—someone who can meet our every need, make us whole, and turn our life around.

However, everyone has shortcomings and a penchant for sin. Pretending otherwise will eventually lead to disappointment. Puppy love is not a mature love, since it is not possible to really love someone before you know them. Ultimately, any successful relationship is built on character, not fantasies. Clear thinking helps, as a divorced relative of mine learned when bemoaning her single status to a friend. To get her to see things more realistically, her friend asked: "Whose husband would you want?" After giving it some serious thought, she decided: nobody's!

Chasing after Romance

It is important to realize that, although there are significant differences between men and women, they actually have even more in common. Each person carries with himself or herself something of the image of God, and everyone is tainted by sin. Every person wants to be valued, to be treated with respect, to be truly loved—and feels a need at some level to reciprocate by extending love to others, including romantic love.

The desire for romance is an integral part of human nature. The romantic impulse is a huge part of our lives—consider how it is used to sell seemingly everything. We long for someone to come along, reach inside of us, and quench some inner desire and show us that we are loved and appreciated. We want someone to be there for us who will be completely committed to us and will always meet our needs. But anyone we meet will just be human. At the deepest level, everyone wants a sense of acceptance, belonging, and security that can only be met by God, our Creator. The temptation is to believe that someone else can do for us what only God can. People want to be loved and accepted, but they make a mistake when relationships, sex, and marriage are viewed as proxies for the love that only God can provide them.

Nevertheless, if the romantic impulse in us remains unsatisfied, it may gnaw away at us. By nature, we tend to focus on what we want but do not have, and this is especially true of romance. Romance is, by its nature, preoccupied with the here and now and tends to focus our attention on the temporal rather than what is eternal. Consequently, we can easily find ourselves "chasing after romance," as if it were something that could be caught. All too often we are fixated on the question "What can this person do for me?" and we get annoyed when someone doesn't live up to our expectations. What we think of as romantic love is all too often just desire or lust: What could be emptier than relating to someone on the physical level without ever knowing them or loving them? But sadly, this is what the world offers us.

True love between people, on the other hand, comes after much time. It grows, and love is ideally the soil in which romance lives. Love doesn't just happen after one conversation, experience, date, or even after a marriage ceremony. Ironically, a preoccupation with romantic and sexual interests inhibits interpersonal growth and communication— prerequisites for a successful long-term relationship.

Looking towards Marriage (Taking the Long-Term View)

While some men and women may actually derive a perverse sense of satisfaction from the manipulative games they play on each other, it remains true that attributes such as honesty and sincerity are what count in terms of day-to-day living in a marriage or in any relationship. What is marriage if it is not two people committed to each other for life? No one *really* wants a long-term relationship based on manipulation and games. Most of those who want to be married, if they are honest with themselves, desire a marriage based on character and unconditional love, which is quite the opposite of what is offered by the self-oriented mentality of the dominant dating culture. However, if a relationship is begun without proper regard for virtue, asserting its importance later is difficult, and increasingly so, the longer a relationship continues without it.

When wedding vows are exchanged, a man and a woman make a promise to each other. They promise to love and stay with each other "till death do us part," for as long as they both are alive—this is the permanence of marriage. This is indeed a "big promise." But any relationship is full of many "little promises" as well: "I promise to be there tomorrow to help you" and "You can count on me to do that." A measure of someone's ability to keep promises on an ongoing basis goes to the heart of what is meant by the words "dependable," "reliable," "trustworthy," and "responsible." It is not surprising that those who exhibit these attributes are much more likely to keep the big promise of staying married. These are not the attributes, however, that come to mind when one thinks of the typical dating relationship. As it turns out, some things that people find attractive in each other while dating are viewed as relatively unimportant (or even negatively) after marriage. For example, while many if not most men initially select a woman based on her physical appearance, most marriages do not dissolve because of unhappiness over the wife's physical attributes.

Our society's pursuit of selfishness has led to much brokenness, leaving us with a culture in which it is all the more difficult to experience loving relationships. As relationships have become more privatized, more selfish, and less family-oriented, marriages are not doing so well and divorce has become common. Dating as it is commonly practiced is a bad proving ground for marriage, and the problems that characterize our dating relationships will carry over into our marriages. The converse, however, is also true: The good habits we practice in relationships before marriage will also manifest themselves in marriage and in all our relationships. Therein lies a tremendous opportunity—it is not an overstatement to say that to the extent we practice unconditional love in our premarital relationships, we chip away at the coarseness of society and change it and the marriage culture for the better.

Dating and Western Culture

The me-centeredness of Western culture, particularly with respect to sexual matters, is a reflection of immaturity; a truly mature person is an outward-looking one who desires to become more loving and more giving, not one who is focused on what he or she can get. Given that the mindset of most is self-serving, though, it is not surprising that the dating culture is predominantly one that is contrived and artificial, with the players being manipulative and deceitful. The fact that this behavior has been largely accepted by Western society as the way that men and women should relate to each other—as *normative*—is an indication of how alienated from God its thinking has become.

Those who cherish virtues, such as honesty and unconditional love, will not feel at home in the dominant dating culture, even if they cannot precisely pinpoint the reason for their unease. Indeed, it is impossible for the virtuous person to be happy about putting his or her interests ahead of others'. Many are uncomfortable with the selfishness that pervades the dating culture but are reticent to express their concerns, thinking that they are alone in their assessment. Dating as it is typically practiced should make followers of Jesus long for a wholesome alternative.

Questions for Reflection and/or Discussion

Have you known people in a dating relationship who loved each other unconditionally? If so, how did they express that love?
How did that love help build their relationship?
Did it make them better people? If so, how?

Have you known people in a dating relationship in which one person was a true friend but the other was selfish? If so, how did that relationship progress?

How do you think the New Testament figure of Nathanael—a man in whom there was "no deceit"—interacted with women of his time?
How do you think he would interact with women if he were living today?

Does the dominant dating culture deviate from God's best for us? If so, how?

Imagine that sin had never entered the world, but instead everything remained perfect. How would relationships between the genders have been practiced?

Does learning to love people in general help us be better lovers of those of the other gender? If so, how?

Is it easier to love God or our neighbor?
Can we do one without the other?

We have a tendency to think about what we can get out of a relationship rather than what we can put into it. Likewise, we prefer to receive unconditional love but are inclined to attach conditions to the love we give. Why?

To what extent might we be trying to protect ourselves (e.g., from being hurt)?

Does attaching conditions to our love come more naturally for us because we live in a society in which people generally interact with each other by exchanging something (e.g., money in exchange for a product)?

PART TWO

Considering Alternatives and History

3

We've Got Attitudes!

Attitudes have consequences.

THERE IS OBVIOUSLY a gap between the values underlying dating, as it is commonly practiced, and the Biblical imperatives regarding love. Christians may feel frustrated and a certain tension, as they are torn between the dominant dating culture and their Christian calling. Questions may arise in the heart, such as: "How exactly should I interact with the other gender?" and "Is there an alternative to the dating culture, something better than this?"

Some Common Responses to the Dating Culture

We may find it easy to reject, on moral grounds, the promiscuity that has become pervasive in the dominant dating culture. But what about the consumer-related aspects of dating: shopping around for a significant other, assigning worth to other people, and discarding someone when it suits us? Here perhaps we are more tentative, both in our assessment of the culture and in how we choose to conduct ourselves.

Unfortunately, we are more influenced by the prevailing culture than we realize. If everyone around us embraces a certain belief, we are more likely to accept it uncritically. Likewise, if those around us accept a certain kind of behavior as normal, we are inclined to do so as well. Small wonder, then, that the dominant dating culture is taken by most people who grow up with it to be a given—a cultural norm that for better or worse is "just the way things are." Even some Christians are inclined to believe that Christianity does not apply to this area of life. Rather, it is just assumed that dating is the thing to do and besides: "If I don't participate, won't I be ridiculed or left out?" Adopting this mindset doesn't resolve the underlying tension, however, since the person who sets aside Christian values and virtue is giving up a sound framework within which to operate. Christians who compartmentalize their life by excluding God's grace and wisdom from their dating life are in an awkward position, particularly if they realize that they are not taking the noblest course of action. Far from being a solution, this approach will generally end up leaving one with a heightened sense of anxiety.

Others try to "Christianize" dating by embracing a softer approach that doesn't break outright with the questionable norms commonly associated with dating but rather settles for modifying them a bit. Being selfish about relationships is thought to be all right as long as it is *balanced* with a dose of "spirituality." Manipulating others or playing games with them is taken to be okay as long as it won't hurt them *too* much. Discarding people—cutting them out of our lives completely—is rationalized as acceptable so long as it is done in the nicest possible way, with *sensitivity*. The hope of such a mindset is that being only partially true to godly principles is good enough, but this is really just an attempt to appease one's conscience.

Still others may become so discouraged or cynical that for a time they become reclusive or avoid the other gender to the greatest extent possible. It seems to them that the cultural situation, as they have experienced it personally, is unappealing and perhaps even hopeless. They basically give up on inter-gender relationships and may feel lonely and frustrated. (Ironically, those who participate in the dating game are also frustrated—precisely because they are part of the game.)

So how do we respond to the dating culture? We should begin by remembering that Christians have a calling—they are to be part of the kingdom of God, a kingdom that is "not of this world" (John 18:36a). The values of God's kingdom and the values of this world are different. If we align our lives along godly principles, we must accept cultural norms only to the extent they conform to those of our God. We need not embrace cultural norms that conflict with our convictions: "It is for freedom that Christ has set us free. Stand firm, then, and do not let yourselves be burdened again by a yoke of slavery." (Galatians 5:1) We are free to do what is right and free to be different.

Many long to find a different approach to relationships, but how do we go about this? Although it is not easy to part with a me-first mentality, a good starting point is to apply the Golden Rule—"love your neighbor as yourself"—without regard to gender. Before attempting to construct any alternative to the dominant dating culture, however, let's consider what the Bible has to say about male/female relationships and how they have been conducted in the past.

Is God Our Matchmaker?

Is there one person God has selected for us to marry? Or, at the other extreme, are we without any divine help when it comes to finding a life partner?

The meeting of Isaac and Rebekah is one instance in which the guiding hand of God was present, and one is left with the strong impression that He did arrange this marriage. Abraham sends off one of his servants to his homeland to find a wife for his son Isaac, telling him that God "will send his angel before you so that you can get a wife for my son from there" (Genesis 24:7b). When approaching the town of Nahor, the servant stops by the well outside the town to water his camels and prays to the Lord:

> "May it be that when I say to a young woman, 'Please let down your jar that I may have a drink,' and she says, 'Drink, and I'll water your camels too'—let her be the one you have chosen for your servant Isaac. By this I will know that you have shown kindness to my master."
>
> GENESIS 24:14

Following this prayer, Rebekah offers to help water the camels, leading to the marriage of Isaac and Rebekah.

Of all the marriages mentioned in the Bible, this stands out most clearly as one in which God's providence was at work. But is the experience of Isaac and Rebekah meant to be the norm? If so, it is curious that the Bible does not include many explicit examples of heavenly matchmaking. While this story clearly demonstrates God's love for His people, it seems to be an exceptional event, especially in light of New Testament teaching. The Apostle Paul wrote: "A woman is bound to her husband as long as he lives. But if her husband dies, she is free to marry anyone she wishes, but he must belong to the Lord." (1 Corinthians 7:39) The most straightforward interpretation of this verse is that God has given us a measure of freedom in selecting a spouse. While it is certainly God's will that, if we marry, we marry a fellow believer, God evidently does not necessarily have a specific person picked out for us, or else the assertion that we are "free to marry anyone" would be a hollow one. Other statements in this letter to the Corinthians also seem to imply that we have a measure of choice:

> If anyone is worried that he might not be acting honorably toward the virgin he is engaged to, and if his passions are too strong and he feels he ought to marry, he should do as he wants. He is not sinning. They should get married. But the man who has settled the matter in his own mind, who is under no compulsion but has control over his own will, and who has made up his mind not to marry the virgin—this man also does the right thing. So then, he who marries the virgin does right, but he who does not marry her does better.
>
> 1 CORINTHIANS 7:36–38

> Don't we have the right to take a believing wife along with us, as do the other apostles and the Lord's brothers and Cephas?
>
> 1 CORINTHIANS 9:5

For those who take comfort in the notion that God has a spouse picked out for each one of us, the idea that we have a measure of freedom in this regard is unsettling. There is, after all, something terrifying about freedom, namely, that we are free to fail, the prospect that we might make the wrong choice. For this reason, some would actually prefer less freedom and, if they could, have God somehow make all their decisions for them. But this is evidently not the way God has designed things. He has given us a measure of freedom, and using our God-redeemed common sense He expects us to play a role in the decision-making process. Of course, this means that other people are free too, for example, free to say no to us, and so there is no guarantee that any one of us will ever get married.

For that matter, there is no guarantee that any marriage will last—that a marriage partner will stick it out, since there is no guarantee that someone will remain steadfast. Unfortunately, many choose to downplay the importance of faith later in life or even give it up completely; if giving up a relationship with God is possible, so is giving up a relationship with another human being. Viewed another way, if God Himself cannot guarantee that someone will be faithful, we can never be sure of, or guarantee, another person's behavior either. (Predicting our own behavior is difficult enough.) It follows that getting married necessarily involves some risk of an unhappy outcome. We can reduce that risk by taking careful inventory of the facts, thinking soberly, praying earnestly, and listening to the counsel of others, but we cannot eliminate the risk inherent in any human relationship, any more than we can program someone to act and think in a certain, predictable way, as if people were like computers. There is risk even when we are convinced that marrying someone is God's will. Even if we have the good fortune of having a matchmaker in heaven, we still must live with that spouse here on earth, and on this side of that great divide there are only fallible human beings marked by sin and imperfection.

As a practical matter, the notion that God is our matchmaker is not necessarily something that people believe in anyway—consider the energy most people invest in looking for a life partner! Curiously, some derive comfort from the idea that God is their matchmaker, but at the same time they feel a need to work hard at finding that special person, so that God's will would come to pass. Consider this: We don't hear people saying that God has "just the right friend" of the same gender picked out for them. Also, friends of the same gender may wonder about where their friendship stands or how deep it is, but they generally don't agonize over it. So why are things viewed differently for friends of the other gender? Probably because there is so much potential for hurt in a male-female relationship and because by its very nature marriage is not meant to be undone, which can be terrifying. So, many comfort themselves with the notion that God has worked out everything for them in advance.

Still others, as if out of desperation, are inclined to believe that any eligible person that comes along is God's choice for them. ("God sent this person into my life, right?") In view of the billions of people in the world, meeting a significant fraction of them in our lifetime is impossible, much less getting to know them. As a practical matter, the choice of a life partner will be limited to those few people we come to know well during the course of our life. Ultimately that is a choice that we must make, unless God intervenes supernaturally and makes that choice for us, as He did in the case of Isaac and Rebekah.

However, even if God does not act as our matchmaker, we ought to remember that He is by no means irrelevant to the process: "If any of you lacks wisdom, you should ask God, who gives generously to all without finding fault, and it will be given to you." (James 1:5) God wants to give us wisdom, to help us think clearly, to keep us from evil, and to be integrated into our lives.

Is There Someone Just Right for Me—a Perfect Match?

Related to the idea that God is our matchmaker is the notion that there is one perfect person for each of us out there, if only we could find him or her. ("Those two are a perfect match!" "You were meant for me!") Imagining that there is one perfect person for us is sentimentality that romanticizes love; it degrades what love really is, namely, *unconditional* love that is not dependent on the "right match." One can even imagine how the idea that there is a perfect person for us could form the basis for leaving one's present spouse for the better, "perfect" spouse. However, there is no perfect mate for any of us, although there may well be one or more right mates. Marriage means sticking with someone for a lifetime, once that choice has been made. This has nothing to do with finding perfection but rather with demonstrating character and commitment.

The notion that there is one and only one special person for us is an idealistic one that can lead to unwillingness to accept another's shortcomings. This is hardly an attitude that is conducive to long-term success in any relationship! In the end, the idea that there is one perfect match for us damages the prospect of having a successful marriage with the less-than-perfect match, and to be sure, every marriage (and every relationship) involves two less-than-perfect people.

Some want to believe that the perfect match will just come along and fall into their life, thereby sparing them any heartache they might otherwise go through. In other words, believing that there is one perfect match for us can be motivated by a desire to be insulated from hurt, failure, and pain, but this too easily leads to abdicating our responsibility in the relationship-making process. But even if there were that perfect match for us out there, would we even recognize him or her? The fact that we can be strongly attracted to someone at one time and to someone else at another time underscores the difficulty in identifying any perfect match out there waiting to be discovered.

In some parts of the world parents still act as matchmakers for their children. It's worth noting that divorce rates are lower in countries where marriages are arranged, perhaps in part because people there have a less idyllic and less selfish view of marriage. Even in the Western world, there are many parents (and others) who on occasion try to act as matchmakers, activity that is not generally well received by the would-be beneficiaries.

As discussed earlier, however, New Testament attitudes towards the subject of marriage point to a measure of individual responsibility. Moreover, it is difficult to imagine how Western society, in which individualism plays such an important role, would ever accept arranged marriages, even if that were preferable. None of us would be pleased with the idea of having someone else make this decision for us. It is, after all, our life being held in the balance, and we want a definitive say in how it proceeds.

•   •   •

Although the New Testament encourages individual responsibility in marriage matters, it also discourages selfishness. We should acknowledge that selfishness (which is often associated with individualism) has led to the mess in which the Western culture finds itself. How we got to this point is the subject of the next two chapters.

Questions for Reflection and/or Discussion

In your experience, to what extent has the Christian community accepted *godly* values when it comes to dating? How has that impacted relationships?

In your experience, to what extent has the Christian community accepted *secular* values when it comes to dating? How has that impacted relationships?

Do you know people who "dropped out" of the dating scene? If so, why did they do that? Were they glad they did? Why or why not?

Does the idea that you have a measure of freedom in picking a life partner make you uncomfortable? Why or why not?

Is it scary to think that anyone is free to walk out of a marriage?
On the other hand, does that freedom carry with it the possibility of even deeper commitment?
Would you prefer a marriage where divorce was not a legal option? Why or why not?

How do you react to the notion of matchmaking? What are the positives and/or negatives to this practice?

4

Relationships a Long Time Ago in Places Far, Far Away

When the past no longer illuminates the future, the spirit walks in darkness.

—ALEXIS DE TOCQUEVILLE

THROUGHOUT THE CENTURIES, men and women have gotten to know each other in different ways. Are there things to be learned from earlier eras, things that we might want to emulate in our approach to relationships? Through books or films, many of us are at least vaguely aware of times that seemed to be happier—or at least less jaded—for men and women seeking a meaningful, romantic relationship. Even the words "ladies," "gentlemen," "courtship," and "modesty" evoke images of eras in which virtue seems to have played a more prominent role, when men and women were more proper and wholesome in their dealings with each other. However, it is easy to romanticize the past—various eras throughout history have also seen difficulties in the area of relationships, difficulties for which we would be reluctant to trade. As we consider what history might teach us, we should bear in mind that while a "good culture" may provide a check on bad behavior and help direct our energy in certain positive ways, it can never change the human heart, which remains unchanged since the fall of the human race (Genesis 3). No cultural system, regardless of how it is constructed, can ever eliminate relationship problems.

Men and women throughout much of the world today engage in some form of dating, especially in Western countries. As discussed in the next chapter, dating is a relatively new phenomenon that arose in America in the early 1900s. It supplanted courtship, which had existed in various forms prior to that. A brief survey of how relationships were made in various pre-American eras will set the stage for considering how American culture has evolved. Although marriage has been practiced in a great variety of ways throughout human history,[1] the emphasis here is on the Hebrew, Roman, Christian, Germanic, and other western European cultural traditions, which have had the most impact on how marriage and relationships are conducted in the Western world, including the United States.[2]

Marriage in Biblical Times

The Bible records many examples of parents acting as matchmakers, all of which are found in the Old Testament. In ancient Hebrew culture, parents played a prominent role in when and who their children married. In the book of Genesis we read the story of Hagar, her son Ishmael, and their wilderness experience in the desert. The story concludes with the words: "While he [Ishmael] was living in the Desert of Paran, his mother [Hagar] got a wife for him from Egypt." (Genesis 21:21) Another story recorded in Genesis 29 tells of the marital pursuits of Jacob, who married Laban's two daughters, Leah and Rachel:

> Jacob was in love with Rachel and said, "I'll work for you seven years in return for your younger daughter Rachel."
>
> Laban said, "It's better that I give her to you than to some other man. Stay here with me." So Jacob served seven years to get Rachel, but they seemed like only a few days to him because of his love for her.
>
> GENESIS 29:18–20

Jacob discovered the morning after the wedding that he had actually been married off to Leah instead, but Laban made amends by "giving" Rachel to Jacob in exchange for seven more years of work.

Even many centuries before Christ, however, the Hebrew culture had changed to the point that parental dictates alone did not suffice, and the Talmudic law required that both the man and the woman to be married give their consent. Also, the practices of polygamy and concubinage (in which a man had one or more concubines, or legally recognized mistresses) died out over time and, in any case, were probably largely confined to the rich.[3]

In Biblical times, the period of betrothal prior to marriage was held in high regard and in some sense was "tantamount to marriage."[4] It represented a clear intention to be married and was not easily undone. Betrothal is evident throughout the Old Testament and is mentioned in the New Testament as well, where it figures prominently in the relationship between Mary and Joseph prior to the birth of Jesus.

The Roman Experience and Early Church Views

Society in the Roman Republic (which spanned roughly the five centuries prior to Christ) was highly patriarchal. According to Philip Reynolds, author of *Marriage in the Western Church*, at least during the early part of the Republic the head of the household "was legally empowered to marry off his sons and daughters, to give them in adoption, and in theory even to sell them."[5] Even in the later Roman Republic, paternal consent to get married was still required.[6] During the course of the Roman Empire (which existed for approximately five centuries following the Roman Republic), the power wielded by the head of the household declined with respect to marriage matters, and the rights of the spouses increased. As explained by Reynolds:

> The rationale for parental interference shifted from patriarchal rights to the need for protection against an ill-considered match. The consent of a mother or other relative might be required, while a father's consent might be considered necessary for the marriage of even an emancipated daughter. In due course, marriages without parental consent came to be regarded as valid, albeit improper.[7]

Significantly, unless both the man and the woman consented to a marriage, it was not considered valid. Parents remained involved in the marriage process in another significant way, by providing monetary assistance to the new couple.[8]

The Church was strongly opposed to divorce, putting it at odds with Roman thought, which was tolerant of divorce while nevertheless recognizing it as less than ideal. By about AD 400, the Church was articulating the position that the marriage bond was fundamentally indissoluble. Over time the early Church made an impact on the surrounding Roman culture, so that, for example, it became more difficult to obtain a divorce under Roman law.[9]

The early Church favored being single over the married state, encouraging Christians to emphasize "spiritual" over physical things. Many of the fathers of the early Church actually tended to look down on sex. The Church maintained this bias towards singleness into at least the Middle Ages. Its views were in stark contrast to those of Hebrew culture, in which celibacy was frowned upon.[10]

When they married, the early Christians did so according to civil procedure: Not until the fourth century were marriages blessed in the Church, and even this did not become standard practice until about AD 1000. Getting married was not viewed as something that happened just in a ceremony, but rather it was viewed as a process. The Church fathers thought of betrothal as "the first stage of getting married."[11] In this respect, they were closer in their thinking to the Hebrews and the Germanic peoples than to the Romans, for whom betrothal was less significant.[12]

The European Experience and Later Church Views

To the north of the Roman Empire lived various Germanic tribes. For them marriage was an even more patriarchal affair than in the Roman Empire, to the point that the consent of the bride was not required when arranging a betrothal. According to Philip Reynolds, Germanic marriage was "a contract of acquisition whereby a man acquires the girl from her family."[13] Over time, the Church largely succeeded in eliminating from Germanic society the practices of relatives marrying each other, concubinage, and polygamy. By the eighth century, the principle of "one wife at a time" was generally accepted in Europe, at least in principle. The principle of indissoluble marriage was met with greater resistance but eventually won out throughout Europe as well. The Church also promoted the idea that both parties to a marriage should consent to it, although the economic realities were such that parental approval remained important.[14]

Marriage practices in Europe changed gradually throughout the rest of the Middle Ages, generally in favor of individuals making their own choices. In their book *Marriage and the Family in the Middle Ages*, Frances and Joseph Gies observed that by AD 1000: "Emphasis had moved away from the old contractual, family-alliance purpose of marriage toward financial support for the new conjugal household. Yet parents maintained control. Marriages were still rationally planned, among peasants as among their betters."[15] In the subsequent centuries, the Church continued to maintain that marriage should be based on the consent of both parties, a view that eventually prevailed in the culture at large. But what exactly constituted consent? Many, especially among the peasants, exchanged marriage vows in private—sometimes with no one else in attendance—and in so doing became married. By the twelfth century, such secret or clandestine marriage had become widespread in Europe. There is evidence that towards the end of the Middle Ages individuals generally had great say in selecting a marriage partner and that some courted. Some even married against their parents' wishes.[16]

This is not to say, however, that people just "followed their heart" when selecting a marriage partner, to the extent that they felt free to do so. Rather, it was the demands of everyday living that weighed heavily on people's hearts. According to Gies and Gies: "The economic function that ensured the family's survival tended to take precedence over other considerations. Marriage partners were chosen to help perpetuate the estate, the farm, or the business; children were an element in the enterprise."[17]

Parents continued to have a strong say in marriage matters throughout the Middle Ages. There were cultural reasons for this, as well as the reality that parents provided a new couple with much needed financial assistance, which often took the form of land. As a practical matter, this might mean that a son did not marry until his father died, or if he married sooner, he and his wife might have to live with his parents. The marriage prospects for non-inheriting children could be difficult, and they might have to save a significant sum of money before getting married. Dowries, whether in the form of money or goods, were important to newlywed couples in the Middle Ages. Whatever form it took, financial assistance from parents to their marrying children was generally needed and had the effect of empowering them economically.[18]

In the sixteenth century, both Catholics and Protestants became reluctant to accept clandestine marriages. There was a growing recognition that society would function better if it was clear to everyone when two people got married. Exchanging vows privately made it easy for one party to back out later and shrouded the marriage with ambiguity regarding its legitimacy. So clandestine marriage was ushered out in favor of church-approved weddings. At the same time, the Church was clarifying its understanding of marriage. Catholics and Protestants both drew attention to the importance of a loving relationship between spouses. Both traditions emphasized the importance of having children, and Protestants in particular promoted the idea that marriage was better than celibacy, which represented a departure from the thinking of the early Church.[19]

The shift away from clandestine marriage to a formal church ceremony brought the process of choosing and marrying a spouse into the open. This had the effect of increasing parental influence but only for a time. Economic changes were under way that favored individual choice in marriage matters. In particular, economic activity was shifting away from the land and towards urban trades. This meant that making a living no longer necessarily depended on one's parents. In addition, the Enlightenment was promoting an idealistic view of the individual and a more secularized view of the world, including marriage.[20]

Driven by these economic and philosophical forces, the old order in Europe gave way to individuals marrying for "love" in the eighteenth century. At the time, some warned that marrying for love could ultimately undermine marriage, since it tended to unduly raise expectations and elevate the notion of personal fulfillment.[21] These concerns became only more acute over the subsequent centuries. In her book *Marriage, a History*, Stephanie Coontz observed:

> In the eighteenth century, people began to adopt the radical new idea that love should be the most fundamental reason for marriage and that young people should be free to choose their marriage partners on the basis of love. The sentimentalization of the love-based marriage in the nineteenth century and its sexualization in the twentieth each represented a logical step in the evolution of this new approach to marriage.[22]

During the last few centuries of the second millennium, these changing attitudes in the West about love and marriage also manifested themselves in premarital relationships, as we will now see.

Questions for Reflection and/or Discussion

In what ways has the Church made a positive impact on the culture of marriage and relationships over the centuries?

In what ways might the Church make a positive impact on the dating culture today?

Was there merit in the early Church's bias towards singleness? Why or why not?

Compared to today, parents in the Middle Ages had greater influence on their children's selection of a spouse but also made significant financial contributions to their marriages. What are the advantages/disadvantages of such a cultural system?

The way people view marriage and their reasons for getting married have changed throughout history. What are some of the "good" and "bad" reasons that people marry today?

5

American Idols:
Courtship and Dating

*The more things change, the more they stay the
same—or do they?*

OVER THE CENTURIES, America has experienced enormous cultural shifts in the area of premarital relationships, with various forms of courtship eventually giving way to dating, which in turn has evolved significantly. Understanding this history will allow us to better understand the current cultural scene and how we can respond to it.

Courtship in Early America

In her book *Hands and Hearts*, Ellen Rothman provided us with "a history of courtship in America," as she described it in the book's subtitle.[1] During the late 1700s and early 1800s, socializing between the genders was conducted differently than in later American eras. She noted that boys and girls met each other in the houses of neighbors and also in community settings such as the village commons, church, and the one-room schoolhouse. The lives of both genders revolved heavily around their livelihood, especially agriculture, and in this way their lives were intertwined. They usually got to know each other in groups:

> When young women and men ventured away from home, it was often in mixed company. They went berrying, riding, picnicking; they sang and danced together at parties and balls and at the singing and dancing schools that were popular in small towns and country villages. One historian of the period observed that "boys took girls for walks, escorted them to college debates and lectures, and congregated at young ladies' homes to chat, eat apples and cakes, and gather around the piano to sing." Male-female socializing did not depend on special occasions but was integrated into the routine of everyday life.[2]

Balls and dances were popular and provided a more formal social setting, but young men and women also got to know each other alone by taking walks, horseback riding, and talking at home.

Marriage was preceded by a period of courtship, which was generally unsupervised by parents. A suitor and his partner often met in the house parlor, since it was one place they could expect to be left alone. After a time, a man proposed, and a woman decided whether to accept. However, marriage was not entered into until the man was financially ready to provide for his future family. This often required receiving a portion of his family's land, so in this way parents often had great influence as to *when* a couple married. Although it was relatively uncommon for newly-weds to take a trip immediately after they got married, when they did so, it often involved visiting relatives. Even when a couple went to a vacation spot, friends or close relatives might come along.[3]

One's spouse was to be both a friend and a lover. Being friends was not by itself considered reason enough to get married, but it was necessary.[4] More generally, "friendship provided boundaries within which men and women could test themselves and each other."[5] The notion of "romantic love" did not make significant inroads into the psyche of the American people until the early 1800s, with romantic attitudes being widely regarded at the turn of the century as immature.[6]

Courtship Goes Romantic

The mid to late 1800s were different with respect to how romance was viewed and its relationship to marriage, as friendship had gradually come to be viewed as relatively less important and romance as more important. Ellen Rothman observed:

> By the 1840s, the process that had begun at the end of the eighteenth century was complete: friendship had been thoroughly devalued and demarcated from love. Phrases such as "mere friendship," "common friends," and "ordinary friendship" appeared—clear evidence that friendship was less intimate, and less desirable, than love.[7]

By the mid-1800s, books and magazines concerned with romance were all the rage, and young Americans came to view romantic love as the only path that led to marriage.[8] The cultural requirement that romance was *the* road to marriage made friendship between the genders less commonplace. At the end of the 1800s, the editor of the *Ladies' Home Journal* lamented that "there is absolutely no half-way station between being a stranger and being a lover. Friendship is never thought of."[9] Going from one to the other required that two people "fall in love." The primacy of romance was now manifesting itself in the period just after the wedding as well. According to Rothman, "by 1880, honeymoon trips to 'romantic' locations were expected to follow weddings. The bridal journey was no longer a ritual designed to integrate a new pair into the community, but, instead, it self-consciously isolated the couple."[10]

Even though friendship had been deemphasized, it was assumed that romantic love should be based on shared interests and that marriage should be based on companionship. Trust, sincerity, and candor were character attributes that were held in high regard, as they had been in earlier eras.[11] However, candor had now taken on an added role during courtship: "In an age that embraced romance wholeheartedly, the great virtue of candor was the counterweight it provided to the idealization inherent in romantic love. Openness would ensure that a lover was loved for himself or herself."[12]

In her book *Searching the Heart: Women, Men, and Romantic Love in Nineteenth-Century America,* Karen Lystra explored the meaning of romantic love to Americans in the early/mid to late 1800s.[13] They believed romantic love was "uncontrollable" and "mysterious," even while recognizing that marriage itself was not idyllic.[14] A romantic partner could be a long-term acquaintance or someone less well known. At least until the latter part of the 1800s, the general pattern was for the man to lead in the courting relationship, while a woman might find a way to encourage a man of her liking without coming on too strongly. Parents were no more inclined to try to pick their children's spouses than their parents or grandparents were, and while it was expected that courting couples would enjoy privacy, they also engaged in group activities with peers. Courtship was characterized by a process of identifying with the other person, in which the parties revealed their true selves and shared their thoughts and feelings about the other.[15]

A Victorian-era courtship that led to marriage generally involved at least one crisis in which the man's love was tested by the woman. For example, she might declare without warning that her personality made them unsuitable for marriage. In doing so, she was seeking reassurance from him that he really did love her—reassurance which, if offered by him and accepted by her, had the effect of deepening their romantic relationship. Once the relationship reached the point that the parties became convinced of each other's romantic commitment, marriage was possible. However, the idea that romantic love was at the heart of marital love but in some sense beyond one's control made it difficult to rebuild love once it had faded. The notion that love could be "undone" contributed to the increasing divorce rates that characterized subsequent generations.[16]

Lystra found commonly held stereotypes of Victorian-era Americans to be at odds with the historical record. While they generally did view the proper role of the husband as that of provider and the wife as that of homemaker (e.g., couples believed that marriage would have to wait until the man was financially able to support the household), they were most definitely not emotionally or sexually dysfunctional. On the contrary, she concluded that men and women enjoyed relationships with each other that were both "intimate" and "emotional."[17] However, sex was viewed as something that belonged within marriage, with both sex and romantic love being regarded as private matters that should not be paraded about in the public square.[18]

If anything, romantic love had become so important that the romantic affections of many were competing with their affection for God, a prospect that had concerned American Christians of previous generations. On the other hand, Lystra opined that romantic love helped make male-female relationships within the American family more egalitarian and less patriarchal, as men let down their guard and learned to identify and empathize with women.[19]

Courtship at the Turn of the Century

By the late 1800s, conventional courtship in America was structured around the practice of "calling," in which a man was invited to visit a woman in her home. In her book *From Front Porch to Back Seat: Courtship in Twentieth-Century America*, Beth Bailey described this practice as follows:

> When a girl reached the proper age or had her first "season" (depending on her family's social level), she became

eligible to receive male callers. At first her mother or guardian invited young men to call; in subsequent seasons the young lady had more autonomy and could bestow an invitation to call upon any unmarried man to whom she had been properly introduced at a private dance, dinner, or other "entertainment." Any unmarried man invited to an entertainment owed his hostess (and thus her daughter[s]) a duty call of thanks, but other young men not so honored could be brought to call by friends or relatives of the girl's family, subject to her prior permission. Undesired or undesirable callers, on the other hand, were simply given some excuse and turned away.[20]

The cultural norms that governed the call itself were complex and addressed such questions as whether refreshments should be offered, and if so, what kind; under what circumstances a chaperone should be present; and what to talk about. Books and magazines of the era kept people informed and well-mannered.[21]

The Advent of Dating

By the early 1900s, dating was emerging and beginning to supplant courtship. Beth Bailey suggested that dating originated in the lower and upper classes and that by the mid-1910s it had worked its way into the middle class. Calling, she observed, was not a realistic option for the lower class, which typically lived in crowded rooms and without a parlor. The upper class, on the other hand, saw in dating a chance to get out and do exciting things. As Ellen Rothman and others have pointed out, the automobile contributed to the shift towards dating by making it easier for young people to get away from home—to be independent. By the mid-1920s, dating—a newly invented custom—had largely replaced courtship in America.[22]

Bailey observed that the shift from courtship towards dating resulted in a significant loss of power for women. In the calling system of courtship, the woman took the initiative by extending a call to a man, inviting him into her home. Dating reversed that: The man was now the initiator, inviting the woman to step away from her turf into public places, where men were dominant. Moreover, it was the man's money that made the date possible, and so the man controlled the agenda. Even more subtle was the impact money had on gender roles. The new cultural norm of men spending money to entertain women led to the widespread notion that a woman owed her date something:

> The dating system promoted sexual experimentation not only through the privacy it offered but also through the sense of obligation it fostered. Dating was an unequal relationship: the man paid for everything and the woman was thus indebted to him. According to many, boys and men were entitled to sexual favors as payment for that debt; the more money the man spent, the more petting the woman owed him.[23]

When young people went out, it was often to restaurants, movies, cabarets, and dance halls, but all these thrilling and exciting activities did not lead to greater openness or communication. On the contrary, as Rothman noted:

A growing emphasis on personality and physical attractiveness made self-exposure a risky proposition. "Catching" a mate had become a matter of wearing stylish clothes and knowing the latest dance step, rather than of demonstrating certain attributes of character…. At a time when young people were expected to woo each other with the right look and the right "line," candor and openness were outmoded virtues.[24]

Getting to know someone of the other gender, much less develop a friendship, had seemingly become even more difficult with the advent of dating.

The practice of dating has undergone significant change over the years. Prior to World War II, the more dates a person had and the more people he or she went out with, the better. There wasn't social pressure for people to form couples; rather, what helped make someone win the popularity contest was to be seen socializing with lots of people, to have many dates with many different people. After World War II, it became increasingly common for couples to "go steady": Rather than dating many different people, a young man and woman would pair off and maintain a *steady* relationship by sticking with each other. Going steady involved staying in close communication with each other and going out frequently on dates, while forgoing dates with others. The agenda for a date typically included some form of entertainment, something to eat, and some amorous activity, in that order.[25]

Dating Goes Sexual

The latter part of the twentieth century witnessed another shift in the practice of dating, namely, its increasing sexualization. Beth Bailey observed in the late 1980s that it had been "more than a quarter of a century since the dating system lost its coherence and its dominance" and that "sex appears to be the normal, if not unproblematic, medium of contemporary courtship."[26] The "sexual revolution" of the latter part of the 1900s was preceded by a shift in standards that had been under way for a long time. There have been various periods in American history when people have been more (or less) virtuous in sexual matters, but one important difference between the twentieth century and earlier American eras was the dramatic change in what the public regarded as right and wrong. When that century began, the widely accepted view (which had been dominant since the first settlers arrived) was that sex is only appropriate within marriage, moral failures to the contrary notwithstanding. Over the succeeding decades, however, the American public became more sympathetic to the idea that sex is acceptable between persons who are engaged, which in turn gave way to the notion that sex is okay between persons as long as they are in love with each other.[27]

Taking things one step further, "being in love" is optional in the way many collegiate men and women relate to each other, as described by Kathleen Bogle in her book published in 2008, *Hooking Up: Sex, Dating, and Relationships on Campus.* She found that the term "hooking up" is itself fraught with ambiguity: Some understand it to mean having sexual intercourse, whereas others say it can refer to just kissing, whereas still others believe it can refer to sexual activity somewhere in between. The initial setting for a hookup encounter is generally a large gathering of friends and/or fellow students at a party or bar. At such a gathering, men and women look for a hookup partner, who may or may not be someone they already know. Sexual interest is communicated through non-verbal means, such as eye contact and/or by paying special attention to someone. If the feelings are mutual, a man and a woman might start kissing right there in public; if they want to take things further, they typically go off by themselves somewhere (e.g., to someone's room). Alcohol is crucial to initiating a hookup encounter, presumably because it lowers inhibitions.[28]

Although a hookup encounter can be the beginning of an ongoing relationship, the most likely outcome is that no such relationship develops. For college hookup encounters that involve sexual intercourse, Bogle noted that almost half of the participants never even see their hookup partner again. Women are especially frustrated by the difficulty in forming meaningful relationships, whereas most men seem happy to move on to the next partner. Contrasting dating and hooking up, she explained:

> College men used to ask women to go on dates with the hope that something sexual, such as necking or petting, might happen at the end of the date. In the hooking-up era, this sexual norm is reversed. College students, following the hookup script, become sexual first and then *maybe* go on a date someday. In fact, going on a traditional style date is likely to happen only if the two partners progress to

the point of deciding to become an exclusive couple (i.e., boyfriend/girlfriend).[29] (Emphasis in original.)

Thus, the hooking-up culture represents a further devaluation of friendship, in that friendship has been further decoupled from sex and romance.

According to Bogle, the hooking-up culture is largely confined to the college campus because of its unique environment. The most important factor may be that students have so much in common: They are demographically homogeneous and often have the same friends, which leads to an "atmosphere of trust and familiarity" that facilitates the hooking-up culture.[30] Moreover, they live in close quarters, view the college years as a time to have fun, have ready access to alcohol and parties, and desire to fit in with the crowd. Once students graduate from college, however, they face a different environment. As a result they exchange the hooking-up culture in favor of more "traditional" dating, in which men take the lead by, among other things, asking the women out and then paying the expenses.[31]

Other Cultural Happenings

Personal ads and online matchmaking services have certainly made their mark and appear to have become a permanent aspect of the culture. Writing in 2011, Paul Hollander made the following observation about personal ads in his book *Extravagant Expectations: New Ways to Find Romantic Love in America*:

In the last few decades, conventional ways of finding a partner for romantic purposes have been abandoned by large numbers of people, including many who are apparently successful, attractive, and well-educated—if their self-presentations are to be believed. This development further illuminates the problems of modernity, especially the decline of community, the growth of social isolation, and the tension between the demands of professional work and emotionally gratifying intimate personal relationships.[32]

The rise of the personal ad evidently reflects frustration with more conventional ways of meeting people and, according to Hollander, is driven by "the desire to escape loneliness."[33] Much the same could be said for the dramatic increase in the use of online matchmaking services, which have taken the personal ad to the next level by making it possible to reach even more people quickly.

Evidently the use of electronic devices is also changing the way people view each other and themselves. Writing in the September 2017 edition of *The Atlantic,* Jean Twenge reviewed extensive statistical data and made the case that the excessive use of electronic devices among those in their late-teen years has actually increased unhappiness and loneliness. Compared to previous generations, they are less likely to spend time with friends and go out on dates, but also less likely to engage in premarital sexual activity.[34]

Where We've Been and the Road from Here

In reviewing the history of courtship and dating in America, various long-term trends—which are necessarily generalizations—become evident. Romance and then sex have been emphasized at the expense of friendship, which has been deemphasized. While a marriage based on friendship and love has in theory been important to all generations of Americans, over time less and less friendship and true love have characterized the relationships that precede marriage.

Consequently, there has been a growing gap between what Americans want in marriage and what they practice before getting married. At the same time, family and community ties have become less important to the premarital couple, with a tendency for the couple to pull away from the larger community or restrict socializing to a peer group. Meanwhile, increasing wealth has made it possible to emphasize the non-economic aspects of marriage, and a life partner is increasingly likely to be chosen with personality in mind and less likely on the basis of character. However, as our expectations of relationships and marriage have increased, so have our disappointments. Our better instincts, perhaps even our conscience, tell us these trends are taking us in the wrong direction. Is there an alternative?

Because the culture has been deconstructed—almost everything, it seems, is up for grabs—those disaffected with the culture now have an opportunity to rebuild it. The Bible doesn't tell us how to date, but it does lay out principles to live by, which can and should guide our thinking and actions. In particular, the great commandments to love God and our neighbor are as relevant today as they were when God announced them. As we think about the dating culture and its history in America, it is hard to deny the need for loving God and others in the context of community, and in particular, the need for friendship as part of a loving male-female relationship. The idea of friendship between the genders is hardly a new one: Augustine suggested that it was central to marriage, and the Stoics in Rome before him likewise emphasized friendship in a marriage.[35] If friendship was considered necessary to couples in early America, when economic and cultural conditions did not favor a casual attitude towards long-term relationships, shouldn't friendship be at least as important to us today? While inter-gender friendship is not a new idea, it is one whose time has come. Ironically, because our society is selfish and superficial, and because a measure of alienation has set in between the genders, developing a true friendship may be more difficult now than it was in the past—not that it was ever easy.

It is not the goal here to attempt to define a set of customs and rituals that a modern-day courtship might entail. Such an undertaking has been complicated by how fractured families have become, and in any case, there will never be a perfect cultural system in this imperfect world, one that could completely eliminate all the tensions and frustrations that might arise in an inter-gender relationship. Rather, the suggestion here is that we follow the great commandments to love God and our neighbor and, in particular, that we build inter-gender relationships around friendship. The norm should not be people being driven first and foremost by sexual attraction, in the hope that someday a friendship might grow out of that, but rather that relationships between men and women should begin with friendship, and that this beginning may (or may not) lead to romance and/or marriage. These ideas, their implications, and what our mindset should be are explored in the following chapters.

Questions for Reflection and/or Discussion

How has choosing a life partner changed in America over time?
Which factors do you think are most important to people today when making that choice?
Which factors are most important to you?

How important do you believe love and friendship should be to inter-gender relationships, including marriage?

Which cultural aspects of previous eras in America appeal to you, if any? Why?

Do the cultural trends described in this chapter seem unstoppable? What would it take to turn things around?

How has the role of women changed as a result of the cultural shift towards dating?
Some maintain that they have been shortchanged over the last century as a result of this shift. Do you agree? If so, how and why did this occur at the same time they were making economic and political progress?

Why is it that so many people are lonely and isolated even as they are surrounded by technology that promises interconnectedness?

PART THREE

A Better Basis for Relationships

Friendship and the Great Commandments

6

How Should We Then Date?

Get ready… Get set… Go—slowly!

THE QUESTION "HOW should we date?" is not unrelated to the question "How should we relate to others in general?" As we contemplate how to construct a wholesome alternative to the dating scene, it is helpful to keep in mind this broader question and also to think about how we ourselves might need to be reconstructed. To the extent that we are better people, all of our relationships will be improved.

The Kingdom of God and Our Perspective on Relationships

As desirable as a romantic relationship can be, it is not the most important relationship we can have, despite the time and effort we might put into it. Jesus makes this clear in response to a question about which commandment is the most important:

> "The most important one," answered Jesus, "is this: 'Hear, O Israel: The Lord our God, the Lord is one. Love the Lord your God with all your heart and with all your soul and with all your mind and with all your strength.' The second is this: 'Love your neighbor as yourself.' There is no commandment greater than these."
>
> MARK 12:29–31

Our priorities and calling are clear: We are to love God, and we are to love our neighbor. These commandments are not independent of each other. God expects us to love our neighbor, but we can love our neighbor most effectively if we have a right relationship with God.

But do these commandments really have anything to do with dating or romance? Yes, because when we take God and His commandments seriously, it changes many things, including how we view ourselves and how we view others, both of which affect our attitudes about dating and how we conduct our relationships.

God wants to change how we view ourselves

As we love God and by His grace learn to love others, we begin to view ourselves differently. We realize that our worth depends on the fact that we are created in God's image and that He has redeemed us—Christ died for us. We understand that our worth does not depend on what other people think of us, and besides, other people are not perfect anyway. So we learn to not take others too seriously and that it is not good to have our self-image tied up in someone else's opinion of us. Likewise, we learn the futility of letting someone else's opinion control our behavior. We become less sensitive to criticism, and even though rejection is painful, we understand that everyone feels lonely and unaccepted at times (perhaps even most of the time), as we consider that Jesus himself was rejected.

As we experience God's forgiveness and acceptance, we become more comfortable with who we are and learn to be ourselves, in the positive sense of the phrase. In the past we may have felt we were not with it (or that everyone else is normal) and asked ourselves: "Why is it only me who is left out and different?" But now we begin to recognize that sort of thinking as silliness and perhaps even self-pity.

As we grow in grace, we see ourselves first as human beings and second as belonging to a gender. As a result, any sense of inadequacy or shame we feel about our bodies may be mitigated. We begin to understand almost intuitively that neither romance nor sex will fulfill us as persons and that some of the best friendships we will have with the other gender will involve the least amount of romance.

God wants to change how we view others

As we love God and by His grace learn to love others, we no longer view other people self-consciously as objects or possible dates. Rather, we see them as human beings who should be loved and befriended (which is not the same as trying to be a friend to an object). We learn to put others' interests ahead of our own. We realize that members of the other gender are first and foremost human beings, who have many of the same struggles and problems that we do.

We are no longer preoccupied with what we can get out of a relationship; rather, we think about how we can enrich the other person's life. We learn that it is possible to have friends of the other gender without all the problems that accompany the dating game, that being genuine and honest are not incompatible with friendship, and that, consistent with the commandment to love our neighbor, we do no harm in being a friend.

As we mature in the Christian faith, we come to appreciate that Jesus died for those at the bottom of the social totem pole as well as those at the top of it—every person is of great worth in God's eyes. Moreover, we learn from the life of Jesus that God is inclined to show even greater compassion upon the downtrodden, the poor, and other undesirables of society. Thus, we realize that those at the top of the social totem pole should, rather than acting smug about their position, make a greater effort to reach out to those who are friendless.

As we learn to view others differently, our views of romance change as well. Whereas we might have been tempted to believe that a romantic relationship need not have much to do with friendship, we come to understand that an *enduring* romantic relationship is necessarily based upon deep and genuine friendship, since the same things that make for a good friendship also make for a good romance. We realize that romance is ideally an outgrowth of friendship, rather than an end in itself, and that although romantic attraction might initiate a relationship, it will never sustain it.

* * *

In short, as we become less focused on ourselves and our life compass becomes reoriented from selfishness (pointing inward) to love (pointing outward), we are in a better position of having healthy relationships, because love is liberating. We become less preoccupied with simply having a good time and become more concerned with leading a good and righteous life. In keeping the great commandments to love God and love others, we are not just better off in theory, but also in practice, because it is in giving that we receive. What matters most is this: knowing God and loving and being loved by others.

Developing Christian Character and Maturity

Friendships go better when we ourselves are better people, so to improve our relationships, we should improve ourselves. As we do, we become easier to live with and find it easier to deal with others. Likewise, if we want to be loved, we should become loveable—a person others would want to be with or maybe even marry. We are more attractive to others when we display self-confidence that is an outgrowth of our faith. Emotional and spiritual maturity should accompany our faith, thereby making it easier for us to love other people. However, if we are not "whole" but instead broken, our relationships will more likely be characterized by pain and rejection. A whole person is more likely to experience a positive relationship than a person who has the attitude: "Here I am—take care of me."

Character is essential to any long-term friendship and is particularly important to romantic relationships because of the temptations that can so easily accompany romance: the desire to use another person to stroke one's ego, the reluctance to give sacrificially when that is most called for, and the urge to wander when difficulties arise. Fundamentally, our character goes to the heart of who we are and what we live for: Do we live by the principle of unconditional love or for ourselves? The answer to this question has a profound impact on our relationships. If we live for ourselves, we are more inclined to manipulate others to flatter our egos, for example. As we learn to give of ourselves as a way of life, however, we move beyond our own insecurities and preoccupation with having others affirm our self-worth.

There are many aspects of a loving character that contribute to a good relationship, including one with romantic overtones. Here are a few that are particularly helpful:

Self-respect: Treat others well but require the same from them

Living by the Golden Rule is not easy. It is difficult to treat others the way we want to be treated, especially those we don't like. However, it is also difficult to insist that our friends treat us with respect. A relationship in which one party (or both) takes the other for granted or does not have the other's interests at heart is not a healthy one. If we let another person take advantage of us, but we don't object, which is usually the easiest thing to do at the moment, we lose self-respect.

Honesty, in things big and small

Someone who keeps promises in "little things" (like showing up at the agreed-upon time) is more apt to keep promises in "big things." Most couples who have been together for a while will structure their relationship in some way that is viewed as a big thing, such as whether they are an exclusive couple or are free to pursue other romantic prospects. However, whether someone keeps "little promises" (and whether he or she follows through on commitments made at work, church, or school) says a lot about that person's character and how likely he or she is to succeed, for example, in marriage.

In any case, a successful long-term relationship is never built on lies—sooner or later the truth will come out. One reason people are not consistently honest is because they are insecure. For example, they are afraid of telling the truth when doing so might jeopardize a continuation of the relationship (and they don't want to lose it) or when doing so might hurt the other person's feelings (e.g., when the romantic attraction is not mutual). "White" lies and manipulative games are a manifestation of this insecurity and are employed to avoid being honest.

Any successful long-term relationship must ultimately be based on authentic self-disclosure and interpersonal communication, that is to say, on reality. Otherwise, one must at some point deconstruct all the pretensions that have been erected in the meantime. To be sure, there is in each of us at least something that is not likable, and parading our faults before the world is not likely to attract many people. However, if we do not present ourselves honestly, we may discover that we have attracted someone—or have been attracted to someone—that wasn't a good choice. How much better it is to live out our lives with integrity!

Patience: Don't be too eager

The longing we have to find romance can, if it is too strong, prompt us to act impatiently and plow ahead, just hoping for the best. In general, it is true that if we want something too badly, our judgment is clouded and we are inclined to settle for second best. This is especially true in the area of romance, where wishful thinking contributes to poor judgment.

Ironically, the person who is willing to do without romance is the one most likely to find a wholesome relationship, just as the person who is willing to stay single is the one most likely to have a happy marriage. We want others to like us, but shouldn't it be important to us that they like us for the right reasons? Because of who we really are? Trying to get someone to like us for the wrong reasons is self-defeating in the end and a waste of time—even if the dominant culture would have us believe otherwise. Being patient allows us to keep high standards for ourselves and for others. We can settle for low standards or hold out for high ones, but only the high road will likely lead to making a good choice of a significant other.

Moreover, to find a suitable match, we should have a realistic assessment of who we are as a person. What are my strengths and weaknesses? Would romance really be a good thing for me at this time? This assessment can take time, since getting to know ourselves is also a process.

Wisdom

It's hard to get too much wisdom or "sanctified common sense," as some have described it. (The book of Proverbs has much to say about it.) In the course of a romantic relationship, decisions (whether spoken or unspoken) are made on an ongoing basis. How will we spend time together today? Looking towards the future, what should be our common goals, and how should we go about achieving them? Viewing such questions through the lens of wisdom can make the difference between happiness and regrets. If we are wise, we will be better able to make good choices in the romantic realm and in choosing a life partner.

* * *

Interwoven through all these character attributes is emotional and spiritual maturity. Gaining maturity is easier said than done, since becoming emotionally and spiritually mature generally does not happen in a vacuum: Unless we experience the love and acceptance of God and of others, our own growth is stunted and our needs as a person will remain unmet. Unfortunately, the typical dating culture is not one that fosters the process of becoming a more secure and mature person. On the contrary, love and acceptance are conditional and rejection is commonplace, so that there is a tendency to become even more insecure and immature over time—a vicious circle.

We do ourselves a disservice, however, if we view maturity as nothing more than a collection of character attributes. We should embrace life and have interests. This world was created, at least in part, for our enjoyment. A person who is engaged in the world and doing God-pleasing things that he or she is passionate about—and not just waiting around for happiness to show up—is someone to whom we are naturally attracted. Bland is not attractive, which is one reason some see the possibility of adventure in the "bad boy" or the "bad girl." Being actively engaged in the world around us and with other people should be the Christian's alternative to being bland.

Developing Friendships in the Context of Community

Consistent with our calling to love our neighbor, we would do well to make friendships based on unconditional love the focus of our relationships, rather than pursuing romance or our personal happiness. (In any case, placing romance before friendship will invariably lead to frustration.) The idea of building relationships on the basis of friendship stands in contrast to the notion that people are only good for what we can get out of them, an attitude that has become commonplace. On the other hand, we do stand to personally benefit from friendships with others, since the lives and actions of others can have a profound impact on who we are and can help us grow as persons. Thomas Martin, author of *The Challenge of Christian Marriage: Marriage in Scripture, History and Contemporary Life*, went so far as to say: "A person has to be loved before he or she can love."[1]

One good setting for developing and nurturing friendships is an outward-looking, service-oriented community of fellow believers, which can be found in many church communities and related organizations. The New Testament actually describes believers in Christ as "brother and sister" and "family" (Matthew 12:50, Galatians 6:10). We should desire, therefore, church communities in which brother-sister friendships are commonplace, rather than the exception. Just like brother-sister friendships within a household, the onus to initiate or sustain a friendship should not fall exclusively on just one gender. A Christian should ideally develop many different brother-sister friendships in the context of community, getting to know and respect many persons as individuals. This may lead to getting to know certain individuals better in view of common interests and shared goals, which may (or may not) lead to a special friendship based on a wholesome attraction for one another. However, it may be that pairing off with someone is not the best use of our time or a good thing for us. (It may even be a negative depending on our situation in life, for example, if we are not ready to face the risks and challenges inherent in a relationship.) And of course, no one should ever become more important to us than God.

To the extent that such communities are loving and encouraging ones, people will feel less compelled to find love and acceptance in the dating world, as if that were the only possibility. Also, a group setting more naturally facilitates getting to know others in a way that is less threatening and less pressure-filled than one-on-one activity. In any case, even the most compatible couple cannot thrive without interaction with other people. Human beings are created such that they reach their potential only in the context of community.

While a church singles group can often be a healthy outlet, it is not necessarily the best example of what a church community should be. By its nature a singles group is limited to a particular demographic group, which tends to promote among its members a narrow view of the world and the Church, while simultaneously making them self-conscious of their marital status. Moreover, such a group is not without its problems. For one, there are those who come to such a group with wrong motives, viewing it as just a dating club. In the worst case, they stick around just long enough to pair off with someone and then withdraw from the group, only to join the group again if they later break off the relationship. ("I'm back!") On the other hand, there are those who would prefer to avoid any romantic relationship in such a group because of the awkwardness that might result if things don't work out as hoped for.

Towards a More Wholesome Progression of a Relationship

Although we would all like to find happiness in the romantic realm, there is no formula for achieving success in romance, and there is no technique lurking out there that will guarantee us a significant other. On the contrary, there is no guarantee that any of us will ever marry or have a happy marriage even if we do. For all of the hype about dating, there are many married couples who never dated in any typical way before getting married. One of my friends remarked shortly after getting married that he didn't know anything more about dating now that he was married than he did before he first met his future wife. Even the Bible suggests that the course of a romantic relationship is imponderable:

There are three things that are too amazing for me,
    four that I do not understand:
the way of an eagle in the sky,
    the way of a snake on a rock,
the way of a ship on the high seas,
    and the way of a man with a young woman.

PROVERBS 30:18–19

While the Bible provides guidance as to how we should relate to each other, the progression of a romantic relationship cannot be reduced to a predefined script. (Besides, who has ever heard of a same-gender friendship that worked that way?) Moreover, how a romantic relationship (or any relationship, for that matter) plays out will depend to some extent on the cultural setting. Nevertheless, the following outlines one way that a wholesome relationship might progress in the event that it leads to marriage.

1. *Meeting others in a group setting*

As mentioned previously, one good place to make friendships is in an outward-looking, service-oriented community of fellow believers. Such a group generally has one or more goals, and the requisite teamwork facilitates establishing many friendships. That's a big plus: If we limit ourselves to being with just one person, our emotional energies tend to be focused on that person, and as a result our expectations may become unrealistic. It is better to meet people incidentally, in the course of doing those things that we would be doing anyway (even if meeting a significant other were not a goal), rather than meeting people just for the sake of trying to find someone special.

While church is one place to meet people, it is by no means the only one. Someone passionate about music is likely to find at least some like-minded believers in an orchestra. The person who is excited about one or more political issues should get involved! Some find the online dating scene attractive because it allows one to screen many people quickly, while maintaining a degree of anonymity and independence. However, it's not called a "virtual world" for nothing: Developing a deep friendship online is a *virtual* impossibility. To move beyond the superficialities inherent in cyberspace, people who meet there will eventually need to meet in person and then would benefit from a group setting.

2. *Getting to know something about each other at a distance*

In a group, we can observe how an individual interacts with other people, thereby gaining insights into personality and behavior that might not be possible through one-on-one interactions alone. How does that individual treat other people, including those he or she doesn't like? A group setting allows us to be tentative and thoughtful in formulating an opinion of someone else, rather than being forced to make a premature evaluation or decision. Is that person really someone we want to get to know better, or are there things about him or her that are disqualifying? What are the things we like and dislike about him or her?

3. *Engaging in conversation, getting to know the other person as a person*

We should take the opportunity to talk with, and learn more about, the other person, without trying to impress him or her. What does he or she believe in? Do we have mutual goals and interests that go beyond a possible mutual physical attraction? We should resist the urge at this stage to pair up and not give into the notion that we have to grab anyone who comes along or risk being left out.

4. *Developing a friendship, occasionally spending time together alone in wholesome, non-threatening activities*

While getting to know people in a group setting is good, it is only natural for friends to spend time alone together at some point, and doing so will likely give them a different perspective of the other person. There is no need to be self-conscious about spending time with someone of the other gender, any more than same-gender friends are self-conscious when they do. It is best that a mixed-gender friendship not be subject to undue circumspection, either by those who are a party to it or by those observing it. It doesn't help that a date is generally viewed as a contrived arrangement between two parties, which usually leads to unrealistic expectations, rather than being viewed as simply an opportunity to spend "extra time" with someone (which is the way a friend of mine said she liked to view it).

It is good to structure time together in a way that is conducive to building a friendship rather than prematurely building expectations, for example, in conversation based on honesty and respect for the other person. To the extent that activities are involved, they should be non-threatening and foster communication. Couples just getting to know each other may benefit more from a walk in a park than from an expensive evening out. When expenses are involved, splitting them equally will diminish anyone's sense of obligation. We should keep our expectations in line with reality and try to put the other person at ease.

5. *Becoming best friends*

Being a person of unconditional love doesn't mean becoming best friends with everyone we meet. As a practical matter, we must be selective. In general, the more two people have in common, the deeper and longer lasting the bond between them will be. In addition to character and a common faith, common interests will contribute to building a friendship.

Is the friendship growing with time? Or are we just learning to tolerate each other? Becoming best friends is no small matter and won't happen instantly. It takes time to develop a deep and abiding friendship, to learn to care about another person (even in bad times), and to understand his or her life and goals. Best friends should be supportive of each other, communicate honestly and candidly, and share an emotional and spiritual relationship, all while being genuine. Becoming best friends involves learning— not just about the other person, but also about how to treat that person and how to be a more loving and mature person—men learning to be *gentle*men, women learning to be ladies.

6. *Considering marriage*

Marriage is an exclusive relationship, so it is only natural that friends headed towards marriage focus more on each other over time. At some point, such a relationship, at least at the psychological level, will not just be brother/sister in nature but will also begin to resemble husband/wife.

The person we marry should be our best friend, but not all best friends should necessarily get married. "Popping the question" may sound romantic, but the decision to get married shouldn't be made lightly. It is a decision that is best made over the course of time, with both parties praying for clear thinking and the willingness to do the right thing (even if that is the hard thing to do), while recognizing that all good gifts are ultimately from God.

Although it is practically unheard of in Western society, there is nothing inherently wrong with marrying someone without having romantic feelings towards that person. Normally one would expect, however, that romance would grow out of a friendship leading to marriage, but at any given time the intensity of romantic feelings may be different for the two parties. Moreover, it is not necessary to go through a string of romantic lovers before deciding on one, as if all that experience were a prerequisite for a happy marriage or would make for a happier one. On the contrary, if that experience involves repeatedly breaking off relationships, it is hardly good preparation for marriage. How much better it is to have had positive relationships with different people of both genders along the way! How well one has loved counts for more than just having known many people well. (To paraphrase Publilius Syrus from Roman times: The person who marries many does not please many.)

Thinking Soberly and Realistically about Both Romance and the Other Person

All things in this world will eventually pass away, even the good gifts of God. One of those good gifts is romance, but by its very nature, romance can preoccupy us. There is a *self* nature to it: Romance tends to focus as much attention on *oneself* as the other person; it is all too easy to pursue romance as an end in *itself*, and it can even lead to *self*-absorption. Having romantic feelings does not necessarily mean that one is in a truly loving relationship and can be the result of nothing more than a particular state of mind. Unlike unconditional love, romantic love is not tied to commitment. "Being in love" with someone and actually loving that someone are two different things. If not accompanied by unconditional love, romance is ultimately self-defeating, because it tends to put the focus on oneself as it is driven on by selfishness. It becomes a problem, rather than a blessing, when it crowds out friendship. Romance can only be expressed in a lasting, wholesome way in the context of unconditional love.

Good looks and a winsome personality—or even good looks alone—can be all it takes to stir the first romantic feelings, but that initial attraction may be nothing more than a sexual one related to hormones, not because that person we just met is necessarily wonderful. As a result of that attraction, it's easy to project our expectations onto the other person and let our thoughts get ahead of where the relationship really stands, but doing so will most likely lead to disappointment in the end. Even under the best of circumstances, romantic love usually fades away.

Time is the enemy of passion, but by the same token getting to know someone takes time. Early in a relationship it is easy to think that we have a clear picture of who someone is, but initial impressions and surmisals are often wrong. Thus, it is not wise to quickly develop a fixed or uncompromising view of someone, whether positive or negative. Likewise, it is good to be sensible when deciding on a level of commitment and resist the urge to get carried away. Becoming preoccupied with the prospect of marriage can undermine the development of a friendship. By taking things one step at a time, we can avoid a lot of consternation and actually get to know the other person better. For those on the receiving end of one-sided romantic interest, rather than dwelling on feelings of awkwardness or giving into the immature impulse to run away, the better thing to do is to take it as a compliment.

For the marriage-minded, the advice of Benjamin Franklin is worth heeding: "Keep your eyes wide open before marriage, half shut afterwards."[2] If we see problems, it's because they are really there, and we can't just wish them away. Is sobriety a virtue? If it is, we shouldn't pretend occasional drunkenness is not a problem or assume that he or she will outgrow it. Is the prudent management of money important? If so, we shouldn't minimize the significance of overdrawn lines of credit. Are we looking for a partner who takes his or her faith seriously? Then we shouldn't ignore a lack of spiritual vitality and assume that we will succeed in changing and/or converting him or her, if and when we get married. If God hasn't changed him or her, how will we? It is ultimately self-defeating to dwell on the prospect of marrying someone we know would not be right for us. And we shouldn't get married because it just "seems like the thing to do"—at the very least, it should be something we really want to do.

It's never good to assume that any particular person is the "best I can hope for." It is tempting to do just that because of the human desire to find someone. If the desire to find a significant other becomes too strong, good judgment can be set aside and result in a poor choice being made, leading to rationalizations and doubts as to whether the right thing has been done and whether the relationship will last. We do well to remember that there are commandments to love, but there is no commandment to be a romantic. We are told to seek righteousness but never to seek romance.

Respecting Each Other

Respect for another person involves appreciating the other person for who that person is and keeping that person's interests in mind. (This, of course, is incompatible with viewing him or her as a sex object.) It is better to be accepting of the other person rather than focusing on changing him or her. We shouldn't demand that someone take a liking to us or expect that person to make us happy. The fact is, not everyone will like us, and everyone has the right to choose his or her own friends.

When two people spend a lot of time together, especially in the early going, it can result in them getting tired of each other. People need to respect each other's space, so we shouldn't be possessive, which the other person might find overwhelming. Being too demanding of someone else's time is usually a reflection of insecurity or low self-esteem and makes us less attractive.

"Ladies" and "gentlemen" may almost sound like terms from a bygone era, but if we're honest, those terms do strike a resonant chord in us. We would all like to be treated like ladies and gentlemen, so in keeping with the Golden Rule we should do the same, by extending courtesies to each other and creating healthy boundaries that facilitate respect. Men should exercise self-control and channel their energies in constructive ways, and women help them do this when they dress and act modestly. These gender roles complement each other, as Wendy Shalit explained in her book *A Return to Modesty: Discovering the Lost Virtue*: Through modesty a woman "invites men to relate to her in a different way, a way that ultimately means that the men win, too, because they are no longer cut off from adult masculinity." She also observed that modesty gives a relationship staying power: "Certainly sexual modesty may damp down superficial allure, the kind of allure that inspires a one-night stand. But the kind of allure that lasts— that is what modesty protects and inspires."[3]

Learning to Communicate with Each Other

Communication makes it possible to understand and get to know another person. Without it, there is really no way for a friendship to grow. In the absence of genuine communication, our understanding of someone will be governed by impressions and surmisals, which may be superficial.

Communication should be built around honesty, transparency, and self-disclosure.[4] Being honest doesn't mean we have to volunteer hurtful comments, but it does mean being truthful. (For example, we shouldn't say "I love you" unless we mean it.) Being transparent doesn't mean we have to spill our guts, but it does mean to live with integrity, to be ourselves, and to not pretend to be someone else. Self-disclosure doesn't mean we have to go out of our way to advertise our shortcomings, but it does involve risk—the risk that as others get to know us, they won't like us as much anymore. On the other hand, their respect for us might grow, which can lay the foundation for a deeper friendship.

In any friendship, misunderstandings are bound to arise. When they do, a frank, positive conversation just might get things back on track, even though the human tendency is to shy away from conflict and confrontation. Resolving misunderstandings is made easier to the extent there is a measure of trust in the relationship.

Avoiding Destructive Thought Patterns

Here are some thought patterns that can afflict people in romantic relationships:

Being obsessed with how the relationship is (or is not) progressing
At various times throughout the course of a relationship, it won't be clear what the other person is thinking or feeling, or how that person views the status of the relationship. Misunderstandings in this regard can most easily arise when two people are just getting to know each other and one person is more enthusiastic about the relationship than the other.

While it is only natural to wonder where things might be headed, thinking about this constantly is not healthy. It is easy to do just that, however, when hopes are raised that Mr. or Ms. So-and-So might be "just right" for us and we want things to work out in a certain way. All too easily we can find ourselves on a treadmill of fretful, seemingly endless introspection, analyzing the latest conversation or get-together for clues about where things stand. A phone call or message is not returned. ("Why not?") Hellos are exchanged, but this time he or she didn't smile. ("Is this significant?") Last week he or she was aloof but now is friendly once again. ("What should I make of it?")

The key to getting off this treadmill is not to give into the urge to read the tea leaves just one more time, which would continue the destructive mindset. Rather, we need to step back and take things in stride, by focusing less on our own desires while learning to live with uncertainty, which is simply part of life. Likewise, when things are going well, it is not wise to trust in the good feelings of the moment to sustain us emotionally. Sooner or later things could change. It is also worth bearing in mind that not every friendship or relationship should be regarded as a possible (or worse, as a probable) marriage. On the contrary, being friends with many people broadens our horizons and helps keep us from becoming prematurely fixated on any one person.

Being self-conscious and nervous

Not surprisingly, being self-conscious is a result of being more focused on oneself than on others. The self-talk says it all: "How am I coming across?" "How could I make a better impression?" "Am I doing what I should do to get what I want?" A self-conscious mindset tends to short-circuit growth in a relationship, precisely because it is focused on oneself. We need to be on guard that our self-interest does not drive our behavior: "Above all else, guard your heart, for everything you do flows from it." (Proverbs 4:23)

While it is common that couples experience nervousness, particularly when they are just getting to know each other, it is not commonly acknowledged that being nervous is generally a consequence of being focused on oneself—a result of a self-seeking mindset that is preoccupied with the moment at hand rather than being focused on a desire to truly love the other person. Although many factors can affect how prone we are to being anxious, being nervous might be an indication of how loving or outward-looking we are at any given moment.

Feeding the mind with lustful thoughts

Lust has never improved a relationship or made for a better person. Whether lust is encouraged by one's own imaginations (e.g., leading to infatuation) or by an external source (such as pornography), it reinforces a self-seeking mindset that crowds out love. Once love has been pushed aside, it becomes all the more difficult to develop a truly loving relationship.

Lust demands commitment—not to a person—but rather to base instincts. By its nature, it seeks self-gratification through the mental manipulation of another person, which is far removed from unconditional love. In effect, it is degrading to the person being used. In the end, though, lust also degrades the person who gives into it. Whenever we ignore our conscience and let ourselves become preoccupied with a fantasy, we exchange truth for a lie, and our sense of self-worth becomes wrapped up in that fantasy. Eventually reality will set in, at which point we may feel empty or even worthless. Ironically, the increased self-centeredness makes it all the more difficult to embrace love and turn back to God, but fortunately God's grace abounds.[5]

"Woe is me!"

When a relationship doesn't work out the way we want it to, or during those times we feel left out, it's easy to dabble in self-pity: "How come everyone else is having a good time?" Ironically, most people probably succumb to this thought at some point in their lives, which means that the lonely hearts have a lot more company than they realize.

Those who run down Pity Lane are not likely to find love but rather a dead end that doesn't lead to the Road to Happiness. Rather than bringing healing, self-pity is more likely to make wounds fester. This is because self-pity is about self, not others, and only by embracing love and looking outward will we find happiness.

The Problem of Rejection

It happens sooner or later to most of us. A few aspects of this problem are considered here:

The pain of being rejected

My grandfather left Sweden as a teenager to come to the United States, where he married and had several children. More than 50 years passed before he saw his country of origin again. While he and his wife were traveling about his homeland, they ran into a previous girlfriend of his, who was likewise much older. So what do you suppose she said when she saw him again? Perhaps something like: "I didn't expect to ever see you again! What have you been doing all these years?" No, the story goes that what she said was: "How could you just run off to America and leave me behind like that?" Fifty years later.

Romantic relationships have great potential for either good or harm. People can be hurt, and the pain can last for years or even a lifetime. Psychologists tell us that many women don't feel worthy of receiving love, so rejection for them is all the more bitter. Rejection can also be a significant factor in a man's thinking, with the fear of rejection keeping many of them from taking much initiative. How we react to rejection and how fearful we are of it are indications of how fragile we are.

Rejection hurts because we want to be loved and accepted. For that matter, rejection is possible in any relationship: Elected officials may later be rejected by the people who elected them; spouses who were once in love may come to reject each other; and even the Creator Himself was rejected by the people He created. Rejection is especially painful in our relationships with members of the other gender, since not only do we feel rejected as a person, but we are also left with the sense that we have missed out on something we really wanted and which, at a deep psychological level, we are programmed to desire. Our sexual nature is an embedded part of our psyche.

When avoiding rejection becomes crippling

When the desire to shield oneself from the possibility of rejection becomes stronger than the desire to be accepted, it's easy to pull back from other people. When this is taken to an extreme, one becomes reclusive—how ironic that the fear of rejection can lead to making the very thing we want unattainable. Unfortunately, cutting oneself off from others, whether completely or partially, inevitably leads to an unhealthy focus on oneself and a downward spiral of negative emotions. Although it's easier said than done, it is better to focus on what we can give to others, rather than dwelling on the possibility of pain and what we might lose.

Reducing the pain of being rejected

We set ourselves up for hurt when we attach too much importance to someone else's opinion. This is especially easy to do if we don't like or accept ourselves, in which case dealing with rejection is all the more difficult. Of course, it is not easy to be secure and tune out the criticisms and opinions of others. Generally speaking, "people are insecure about themselves and insecure about each other," as a friend of mine put it.

The support of our Heavenly Father and caring friends here on earth is a big help when one is rejected. For this reason, having a positive, growing relationship with God and other friends is a good thing when beginning a relationship that has romantic overtones, in which the potential for hurt and disappointment is great.

Dealing with others in view of rejection

Because a romantic relationship can end in pain, it behooves us to be careful in our dealings with each other. We need to be mindful that others are human beings too and to keep their interests in mind. Thus, it is good to be tentative in forming a romantic bond, knowing that the outcome is often not a happy one for either party. When the vices of romance or sexual desire gain the upper hand, friendship is often the loser; only infrequently do we hear of a couple putting a romance on hold so as to not damage the friendship. Also, a romance that progresses too quickly and moves ahead of the friendship can lead to uncertainty about the future of the relationship. The response to the ensuing emotional turmoil can be to break up, which is often viewed as the simplest solution, even though it is not necessarily the easiest or best one.

"Breaking Up" and Other Possibilities

A platonic friendship may wax and wane, but it normally doesn't end badly in the absence of some sharp disagreement. On the other hand, the term "breaking up" is used almost exclusively in connection with romantic relationships, indicating that we view them differently. It is a vivid description—the *breaking* of something that had been previously viewed as positive or even wonderful. That "something" is usually not just the romance but any friendship that had accompanied it—a *breaking* of the entire relationship.

How sad it is when a friendship, which began with high hopes, completely disintegrates! It is difficult to reconcile such an outcome with the Biblical imperative to love one's neighbor. Someone fails a friendship when the parties cannot at least remain on cordial terms. That "someone," to take an extreme example, might be a physical abuser who makes the continuation of a relationship unfeasible. The point is not to condemn everyone who has been a party to the breakup of a friendship that gave way to animosity, since not everyone is responsible for such an outcome.

However, breaking up with hard feelings is not the only possible outcome when a romantic relationship reaches a difficult point, such as when there is uncertainty over how it might continue or even the desirability of it continuing. Several are listed here in order of increasing emotional stress:

- Living with the uncertainty for a time, without forcing the issue, and while focusing on God and keeping the other person's interests in mind.
- Engaging in a friendly discussion in which things are talked out. There are risks here—the relationship may never be quite the same again, and there is danger in forcing the issue if it would be better to wait for a more opportune time.
- Pulling back and reevaluating the relationship, while spending less time together.
- Parting company on amicable terms. This might involve a mutual understanding that the parties are not good for each other. In difficult situations, this might involve a cordial but uneasy truce between the man and the woman.

We would do well to remember the admonition from the Apostle Paul: "If it is possible, as far as it depends on you, live at peace with everyone." (Romans 12:18)

The Helpful Perspective of Friends and Mentors

Everyone needs friends and mentors to grow as a person— that's the nature of human experience. Without them, we will likely have significant misconceptions about ourselves and perhaps the other gender. Friends and mentors can help us keep a proper perspective, since in general we don't see things objectively, especially when we are preoccupied with romance. We just might learn a lot about a prospective partner through the eyes of another person. For those who are romantically involved, having a confidant to whom we can be accountable can help us stay on the straight and narrow. Unfortunately, people are often lonely and isolated, so real friends and mentors are often scarce.

We should be no less a part of a larger community just because we have a significant other. To the extent that it is possible, this community should also include parents and other relatives. Parents, relatives, and friends all play an important part in most wedding ceremonies. We want their blessing, which is one reason we invite them to the wedding. But if we want their blessing at the ceremony, why not covet it before? Since we get married in the presence of others, it only makes sense that others be present in our lives before the big day.

When Choosing a Life Partner

A life partner should be someone who shares our outlook on life. For the Christian, this means above all a serious faith, a desire to know and love God. Although friendships with non-Christians can be meaningful, and every Christian should maintain friendships with non-Christians, there is something that a Christian and a non-Christian will have a difficult time sharing together, namely a common understanding and appreciation of God, His presence, and His working in one's life. This is why a romantic relationship between a Christian and a non-Christian will generally end in frustration for the Christian. The Christian longs for a deeper relationship with the non-Christian that includes spiritual communication, but he or she knows that this won't become a daily reality unless the other person comes to accept the same faith.

Although we may give intellectual assent to the idea that a life partner should share our basic religious convictions, we must realize—and to some extent be on guard against the possibility—that we will be attracted to those who do not share those convictions. That this attraction happens should not surprise us, since God created men and women so that they are attracted to each other. It is possible, even easy, to fall in love with those who do not share our faith. They too are created in the image of God, and many of them are nice and attractive people. Romantic feelings can be easily awakened, which can lead to problems, for example, when one person desires marriage while the other either does not or is willing to marry only against his or her better judgment.

Of course, a shared faith by itself won't guarantee a happy marriage. If it could, any two Christians who married would be on their way towards marital bliss. Choosing a life partner wisely means giving due consideration to many things. Do we have common life goals and spiritual goals? Do we have common interests? Do we have the same values with respect to money and giving? Do we want children, and if so, how many? Do we complement each other's strengths and weaknesses? These are not questions that preoccupy us when we first meet someone we like. However, working through these and other questions honestly—even though it may be difficult—may be crucial to a successful marriage.

Those headed towards marriage should keep in mind that it is not a panacea or a cure-all. Moreover, those who enter into marriage should do so with the understanding that it is meant to be permanent. Marriage is designed to be—and certainly can be—a great blessing, with God going so far as to liken marriage to His relationship with the Church. Small wonder then that people continue to get married—even if they don't live happily ever after.

Questions for Reflection and/or Discussion

Do you know of a married or engaged couple whose pre-marital relationship stands out in your mind as being admirable? If so, how did they distinguish themselves?

Can you think of a relationship that would have turned out differently had one or both parties been more mature? If so, how did their relationship play out over time?

Have you known of a couple who married quickly but still had a satisfactory long-term relationship? If so, why do you think it worked out?

Has God's influence in your life changed the way you view relationships in general? If so, how?

Has God's influence in your life changed the way you view inter-gender relationships? If so, how?

Imagine a world in which there were no social groups but instead just individuals forming one-on-one friendships with each other. How would the lack of any social groups affect the nature and quality of those friendships?

In his book *Extravagant Expectations: New Ways to Find Romantic Love in America,* Paul Hollander opined: "Electronic communications may also become a substitute for meeting and interacting with flesh-and-blood human beings."[6] Do you agree with this assessment? Why or why not?

7

Being Sexually Pure in an Impure World

When all else fails, read the instruction manual.

THE WORLD DIDN'T start impure, and sex was not something Adam and Eve invented when they were in a dirty mood. A lot has happened since the world began, however, and sexual impurity is all around us in this "modern" world of ours. We are exposed to sexual images through various media, which tempt us to accept and even dwell on things that our better instincts regard as unthinkable.

Since sex was created by God out of love for His Creation and was intended for good, it would be foolish to ignore what He has to say about it. Unfortunately, that is precisely what many have done, and the cultural brokenness around us is perhaps nowhere more evident than in the sexual arena. To get back on track, it has been said that we should view the Bible as the appropriate instruction manual, which was written by our Creator who redeemed us.

Sex and Our Relationship with God

In the book of Genesis, God makes it clear that He created sex with maleness, femaleness, and a loving marriage in mind. Sex was never intended by God to be an end in itself or viewed as an isolated act. Jesus is recorded in the book of Matthew as saying:

> "Haven't you read," he replied, "that at the beginning the Creator 'made them male and female,' and said, 'For this reason a man will leave his father and mother and be united to his wife, and the two will become one flesh'? So they are no longer two, but one flesh. Therefore what God has joined together, let no one separate."
>
> MATTHEW 19:4–6

By God's design, sex finds meaning between a man and a woman in the context of marriage, where children and a larger family are usually not far behind. Through the wonder of procreation, God allows others to come into being, who in turn are able to experience both God's love and the love of other human beings. Although the dominant culture has tried to decouple sex from marriage, children, and even human relationships, the result has been the impoverishment of all of these, the degradation of sex, and frustration for all concerned.

God not only proclaims that there is a right place for sex but also a wrong place for it, where it brings harm: "Marriage should be honored by all, and the marriage bed kept pure, for God will judge the adulterer and all the sexually immoral." (Hebrews 13:4) Moreover, God desires that everyone lead a holy and honorable life:

> It is God's will that you should be sanctified: that you should avoid sexual immorality; that each of you should learn to control your own body in a way that is holy and honorable, not in passionate lust like the pagans, who do not know God; and that in this matter no one should wrong or take advantage of a brother or sister. The Lord will punish all those who commit such sins, as we told you and warned you before. For God did not call us to be impure, but to live a holy life. Therefore, anyone who rejects this instruction does not reject a human being but God, the very God who gives you his Holy Spirit.
>
> 1 THESSALONIANS 4:3–8

Clearly, the measure of a person's worth is not how many different sexual experiences he or she has had, nor are such experiences a recipe for happiness. On the contrary, sexual sin can easily lead to a vicious circle of guilt feelings and moral failure, bringing to mind the lament of the Apostle Paul regarding the law and sin: "I do not understand what I do. For what I want to do I do not do, but what I hate I do." (Romans 7:15) However, lest any despair, there is forgiveness for those who turn away from sin: "If we confess our sins, he is faithful and just and will forgive us our sins and purify us from all unrighteousness." (1 John 1:9)

Just as sex is a gift from God and says something about His love towards us, so too does our sexual behavior say something about our love for God. Jesus said: "If you love me, keep my commands." (John 14:15) It is when we are tempted to give in to selfishness that our character is tested and we show ourselves to be who we really are. Consider the Old Testament figures of Joseph and Samson and how they handled their respective situations. Whereas Joseph went to great lengths to keep himself pure in the matter of Pharaoh's wife and was blessed by God for it (Genesis 39), Samson gave in to Delilah's temptation and suffered as a result (Judges 16). Unfortunately, many don't take Biblical admonitions seriously until they get burned as a result of ignoring them.

There are many rationalizations for engaging in sex outside of marriage. In the moment of temptation, we may wrestle with thoughts, such as: "Why not just go ahead and do what my body is urging me to do? I know God doesn't approve, but He'll forgive me. Sure, there could be some pain as a result of giving into temptation, but I'll get over that, and it's so much more fun to pursue the moment. Besides, all sin is the same, right?" As an initial matter, not all sin is the "same":

> Flee from sexual immorality. All other sins a person commits are outside the body, but whoever sins sexually, sins against their own body. Do you not know that your bodies are temples of the Holy Spirit, who is in you, whom you have received from God? You are not your own; you were bought at a price. Therefore honor God with your bodies.
>
> 1 CORINTHIANS 6:18–20

The consequences of sexual sin—or any sin, for that matter—may haunt us for a long time. In the Old Testament, we read of King David and his adulterous relationship with Bathsheba (2 Samuel 11). Even though God forgave him, negative consequences resulting from his behavior followed him the rest of his life. Furthermore, when we engage in sex outside of marriage:

- We settle for a short-term relationship rather than one that requires long-term commitment (i.e., a marriage commitment to someone special), and in so doing we settle for something less than what God wants for us.
- We are hoping in advance that God will clean up the resulting mess and that somehow everything will work out okay in the end.
- We ignore the fact that disobeying God is not a good way to get to know either Him or a friend.
- We set aside our relationship with God and elevate a human relationship above it.
- We cheapen ourselves and become less desirable.

It is sobering that many self-professing Christians who choose to go down the path of sex outside of marriage never find their spiritual bearings again and essentially give up their faith. Writing in the November 2010 issue of *Christianity Today*, Drew Dyck observed that "moral compromise," including sexual indiscretion, is often a factor in young people deciding to leave the Church:

> A teenage girl goes off to college and starts to party. A young
> man moves in with his girlfriend. Soon the conflict between
> belief and behavior becomes unbearable. Tired of dealing
> with a guilty conscience and unwilling to abandon their sin-
> ful lifestyles, they drop their Christian commitment.[1]

A broken relationship with God—broken off in the worst
case for a lifetime—is a high price to pay for sexual immo-
rality and raises the question: Is it really worth it?

Sex and Our Relationship with Others

Our behavior in sexual matters speaks not just to our love
of God but also to our love for other human beings. By
abstaining from inappropriate sexual behavior before marriage, a couple—if they do marry each other—will build
confidence that inappropriate extramarital behavior will
not take place after they get married, which is a blessing.
Similarly, if they do not marry each other, they show respect for each other's future spouses and contribute to
those future marriages by sparing them the psychological
scars that would otherwise arise from a previous sexual affair. In this sense, then, keeping ourselves pure before
marriage is love that is extended towards future spouses
and true to the Golden Rule. It is love that is extended to
the larger Christian community as well, since its reputation
and well-being are damaged by any sin, including sexual
sin. On the subject of sex and community, William Cole
made the following insightful observations at the dawn of
the American sexual revolution in his book *Sex and Love in
the Bible*:

Sex involves relationships, and the Bible is centered in relationships.

Not only does sex relate to the individuals concerned, in their inner, psychic lives, but also to the nexus of community in which those persons are involved. No parent is indifferent to the sexual experiences of his child; no married person regards the activities of his or her spouse casually; no close friend is uninvolved in the risks and problems of those bound to him by the ties of affection. These lines of community, of relatedness, are obscured by much current discussion of sex, which centers only on those immediately concerned, or the couple *in vacuo*. But no couple is ever isolated. The inescapably interpersonal character of all life is a note the Bible strikes again and again, from the Old Testament stress on the family and its demands, the community and its concerns, to the New Testament assertion that "we are members one of another." We are caught in a network of mutual responsibility, in the biblical affirmative to Cain's ancient question, "Am I my brother's keeper?" Every sexual act, therefore, draws into itself the total personalities of the two human beings participating, and also those to whom they are bound in kinship and affection.[2]

Cole offered a positive assessment of sexual fidelity within marriage when he described marriage as "a lifelong covenant which carries with it a depth of satisfaction and community that is simply unknown to those whose sexual experience is casual or commercial."[3]

The dominant culture's view of sex and relationships, in which people are considered disposable, does not square with the Biblical one. As a pastor I knew, Ron Simkins, put it:

> Persons are not to be treated as things. Sexuality is never to be seen *just* as part of the "natural" cycle. Sexual expression is an opportunity to know God and to know and be known by another human. To *use* someone is wrong, to use and then *discard* them is atrocious! This is the ultimate attempt to be the godlike center of the universe and the ultimate desecration of God and man (male and female, cf. Mal. 2:13–16 and Amos 2:7–8).[4] (Emphasis in original.)

Men and women impoverish their relationships with God and their fellow human beings when they lower their standards in sexual matters. Our behavior should reflect the character and glory of God, not selfishness. However, sex outside of marriage is driven not by a desire to give but rather by a desire to get without commitment—the opposite of loving your neighbor. So we see that God's commandments are meant for our good. How much better it is to show respect for oneself, others, and God by saying yes to sexual purity.

The Stupidity of Fornication

Both men and women do something stupid when they commit fornication. This doesn't mean, however, that everyone who does so is a stupid *person*, since anyone is capable of doing stupid things.

Women, perhaps more so than men, want to be cherished and loved. Some are inclined to think that giving a man sex will get them something meaningful in return. My mother must have had this in mind when she used to tell her children (all boys): "When a girl has sex before marriage, it's stupid first and sinful second." She didn't mean that different standards of morality apply to the genders; rather, she was alluding to the different mentalities that men and women have. Unfortunately, some women think that by having sex before marriage, they can somehow "capture" a man or at least deepen the relationship. Ironically, the woman herself might even prefer to forgo sex, but she thinks that by engaging in it she is somehow contributing to the relationship. Men, on the other hand, are less inclined to believe that love and sex are tied together—if they thought that way, prostitutes wouldn't have any customers. Nor does an unmarried man who is pursuing premarital sex necessarily do so with the expectation that it will nurture a relationship, in spite of what he might tell his girlfriend. So men and women think differently about the connection between sex and love.

Unfortunately for both genders, sex outside of marriage cheapens a relationship. What the woman in particular wants—a deeper, long-lasting relationship—becomes either impossible or at least less likely when she gives in to her boyfriend. It is a stupid thing to do. Sex won't improve the relationship in any permanent way or change her boyfriend's mentality on the subject of love and sex. A woman may think that she can use sex to hold onto her boyfriend, but the reality is that the woman who engages in sex before marriage typically goes through a number of sexual partners before marrying (if she ever does), and so she really isn't holding on to anything. She is giving herself away and getting no guarantees in return. Whether at the most fundamental theological level it is possible for something or someone to be "stupid first and sinful second" is something to ponder. Perhaps the order (stupid and then sinful) is intended to shock us a bit. The proverb I heard from my mother says to women who are tempted to lower their standards: "Even if you suppose that there is neither a God nor a need to follow His commandments, it is stupid to commit fornication, since you won't even get the very thing you most desire, and you will be giving away for nothing something you already have."

Few men are inclined to believe that they could captivate a woman through bed gymnastics or that extramarital sexual activity could deepen or improve a relationship in any lasting, meaningful way. Nevertheless, a man is likewise doing something stupid when he engages in sex outside of marriage. He is not considering the negative consequences of his actions, which include damaging the woman he claims to love, himself, and their relationship. Indeed, at the moment he feels compelled to have sex he is not thinking clearly at all. He is driven by hormones—not reason, maturity, or love. I once knew of a man who had been living with his girlfriend for some time, but in the end he decided not to marry her, because he had always "wanted to marry a virgin" and of course by then she wasn't. (How did that happen?)

In addition to damaging people and their relationships with God and each other, sex outside of marriage can lead to other outcomes, such as procreating a life (with all the responsibilities that entails) and contracting diseases. Imagine: a few minutes of fun in exchange for regrets that can last a lifetime. A consumer item having those characteristics would likely be subject to lawsuits. And yet the lure of extramarital sex is that there is something to be had for nothing, even though our objective experience tells us that everything in life that is worth something costs someone something.

All things considered, engaging in sex outside of marriage is a stupid thing to do.

How Far Can I Go?

Romantic love involves passionate affection for, and a desire to be with, another person, to the exclusion of others. However, there is a dimension to romantic love related to self-gratification, with one example being sexual relations, in which the desire to be joined with another can coexist with the desire to please another. By its very nature, then, romantic love is in part self-conscious or focused on oneself, which can give rise to tension between selfless love for another and self-interest. To make matters more complicated, romantic love as it was created has been corrupted by selfishness. As a result, it is easy for one's thinking to be preoccupied with that aspect of romance that is self-conscious, resulting in a romantic relationship characterized by selfishness. Unfortunately, romance can become an end in itself or even a dead end, and romance ahead of its time is like the proverbial cart before the horse.

The question "How far can I go?" and similar questions are all too often asked with another question in mind, namely "How much can I get away with?" In this case, the answer to the former question is "You've *already* gone too far," because the question is motivated by selfishness, not by love for one's neighbor. (It's interesting that few people agonize over the question: "How much love for my neighbor would be too much?") The person who asks the question "How far can I go?" should pause and ask himself or herself what the purpose of the relationship is. Is it to build and nurture a friendship, or is it something else? Someone who is serious about building a friendship should not be focused on what he or she can get away with but rather on what he or she can contribute. Someone who is focused on romantic or sexual favors is not counting the other person better than himself or herself. Such an attitude can even manifest itself in pressuring the other person to give in to certain physical activities, but this is hardly characteristic of unconditional love.

A relationship is out of balance when physical activity hinders the development of the friendship. One clear warning sign is when the physical activity becomes habit forming. Many find it all too easy to emphasize the romantic or physical aspect of a relationship to the detriment of genuine communication: Engaging in passionate activity and conducting a meaningful conversation are generally mutually exclusive. Also, being uncomfortable about the level of physical involvement is usually a cue that there needs to be more communication.

So should any physical expression of love precede marriage? If so, what limits to physical involvement are appropriate? Physical manifestations of love occur naturally between friends and relatives. Thus, to demand that no physical expression of love occur between two people who are in love would be dehumanizing. However, we know instinctively that some kinds of touching outside of marriage can be problematic, such as those that are sexually arousing. Nevertheless, there is a difference between that which is *sexually arousing* and that which is *merely tender and affectionate*, which is ideally what should characterize the romantic love of unmarried couples. Although the dividing line between the two may be different for different people, expressing affection (for many, hugs and holding hands would fall into this category) is generally accompanied by contentment and the warmth of friendship, whereas sexually arousing activity (certain kinds of touching) drives one towards more.

No romantic relationship outside of marriage will suffer if sexually arousing activity is avoided. Here are a few of the benefits:

- You'll get to know the other person better.
- You'll be more likely to build respect for, and learn to care about, the other person.
- You'll see yourself, the other person, and the relationship more objectively.
- You won't be as likely to get married because of a hormonal rush.
- You'll have a clear conscience. Passionate feelings can temporarily crowd out qualms of conscience, and repeatedly doing something that is wrong tends to break down healthy psychological inhibitions.
- You'll be less likely to hurt the other person. Ironically, momentary pleasure can lead to a broken relationship and pain.

It is best to avoid physical activity that results in loss of self-respect, loss of respect for each other, or even to emotions that feed upon themselves, since emotions and feelings can too easily become one's focus and crowd out the friendship.

Various guidelines have been proposed in an attempt to codify what sort of behavior is acceptable and will keep us out of trouble. A college friend of mine was fond of saying: "Don't let your lips get ahead of your heart!" It brings to mind the story of Billy Graham and his future wife, Ruth, who did not kiss on the lips until they were engaged.[5] Another maxim that has been suggested is "Stay vertical!" The point is that as long as your body is aligned vertically with respect to the ground, it is difficult to go too far, whereas spending time horizontally (on a bed, for example) represents a geometrical alignment that can easily lead to regrets. One might even rephrase this advice as follows: "Stay upright!"—a play on words that alludes to a physical orientation as well as a moral attitude, both of which will help keep us out of trouble. Staying upright morally includes guarding your mind from impure thoughts and choosing your friends carefully.

Setting limits to physical activity can be liberating and provides parameters within which a friendship can grow. It's important to decide on those limits ahead of time and stick with them. Many have also benefited from having a friend in whom they can confide and to whom they can be accountable. Another good idea is taking time out with God to consider how we would react in the moment of temptation and asking Him to "deliver us from evil." As the Apostle Paul wrote:

No temptation has overtaken you except what is common to mankind. And God is faithful; he will not let you be tempted beyond what you can bear. But when you are tempted, he will also provide a way out so that you can endure it.

1 CORINTHIANS 10:13

The Challenge of a Sexually Impure Culture

Admittedly, a difficult road lies ahead for anyone who wants to be virtuous in sexual matters or, for that matter, in any realm of life. There are temptations all around us that would lead us astray, there are many voices encouraging us to do the wrong thing, and there are no longer cultural restraints on behavior to the degree that there were a few generations ago. On the contrary, the dominant culture would have those who are virtuous be ridiculed to the point of embarrassment.

As it turns out, one reason the dominant culture is dominant is because others are convinced it is. Kathleen Bogle found that many college students had the false impression that "everybody's doing it."[6] She went on to say: "Students' perceptions of their classmates, whether accurate or not, are important because it affects their own behavior…. In some cases, students' perceptions of the norms for their peers seemed to make them feel pressure to conform."[7] And no doubt there are some who believe that what other people are doing must be okay, provided enough of them are doing it—a morality determined by the majority, so to speak. Thus, to the extent that the behavior of students (or people in general) conforms to their perception of the dominant culture, this perception drives reality and the culture is worse as a result. By the same token, however, the culture could be changed simply by the non-conformists coming out of the closet and speaking up, so that everyone—in particular those on the fence—would be encouraged to do the right thing. The words of Jesus come to mind:

> Neither do people light a lamp and put it under a bowl. Instead they put it on its stand, and it gives light to everyone in the house. In the same way, let your light shine before others, that they may see your good deeds and glorify your Father in heaven.
>
> MATTHEW 5:15–16

God would have us be a light to others, but remember that light often has a way of attracting moths—so expect to be ridiculed for doing the right thing. Yes, with God's help anyone *can* choose to do the right thing.

Questions for Reflection and/or Discussion

Does the "sexual freedom" of this world—in which people are encouraged to constantly give into their desires—seem liberating, or is it more akin to an unhealthy addiction? Why?

Do you think people relieve sexual tension by engaging in fornication, or does doing so just drive them on towards more?
How does fornication affect people?

What was God's reasoning behind His commandments regarding extramarital sex? That is, what is the point of these commandments?

Imagine a world in which there were no extramarital sexual affairs. Would that be a better place to live? If so, in what ways?
In general, would people in such a world be more inclined or less inclined to trust each other (e.g., in non-sexual matters)?

All other things being equal, would you prefer to marry someone who had never engaged in extramarital sex or someone who had done so? Or would it make no difference? Why?

All other things being equal, what if the choice was between someone who had engaged in one extramarital affair and one who had engaged in ten?

If you were married to someone who had been sexually pure before marriage, would that conduct tend to increase your confidence in him or her? Why or why not?

If you were married to someone who had not been sexually pure before marriage, would you feel a need to forgive him or her for previous sexual indiscretions, even if those had occurred before you met? Why or why not?

Do you see benefits in abstaining from sex before marriage? If so, what are they?

AFTERWORD

Looking Forward to Counterculture

It may be that the day of judgment will dawn tomorrow; only then and no earlier will we readily lay down our work for a better future.

—DIETRICH BONHOEFFER[1]

FOR CENTURIES ECONOMIC changes have altered how marriage and relationships are conducted. Marriage was once driven largely by economic and family considerations, but in modern times it has become more of an individual affair. The economic independence, cultural freedom, and leisure time enjoyed by the modern individual, all of which have been made possible by greater wealth, have even made the pursuit of the "dream mate" commonplace. This desire for self-fulfillment has led to a gap between what is desired in marriage and what a marriage can realistically offer—an expectations gap that can easily lead to marital discord or even divorce.[2] What is more, higher standards of living have made it easier—economically speaking—to get divorced, as some no longer perceive a compelling financial reason to stay together. Premarital relationships have likewise come to be viewed as a self-oriented matter, with people being free and even encouraged to do as they please. The unintended consequences of wealth at least partially explain why relationships are less stable than they once were. In this sense, one could argue that, at least in recent history, the creation of ever greater wealth has contributed to the destruction of our culture.

Wealth and technology are not bad in and of themselves. On the contrary, if they are used wisely they can be great blessings. People now live longer lives, often free from hunger and once-dreaded diseases. They have more time for serving others, learning, and reaching their potential. People now have the ability to do what they want, more so than ever before. However, what people do and what is good for them are not always the same. With opportunity and cultural freedom comes a commensurate need for responsibility, for making wise choices: For those who have the character and maturity to make responsible choices in the matter of relationships, this may well be the best of times, but for those who make irresponsible choices in their dealings with others, this just might be the worst of times. Ironically, there seems to be a decline in responsibility at the very time it is needed more than ever before, and it is hard not to believe that our culture is in decline, in the matter of relationships and otherwise.

Unfortunately, the influence of God, the Church, and the family is waning in the West, even though these are all needed to help us out of our predicament. It is remarkable that over the millennia no one has ever found a satisfactory substitute for any of them, even after experimenting with so many alternatives. Some may long for a technological solution to the current cultural decline, but there is none to be found: Higher standards of living are not leading to higher standards of loving. This is because in the matter of marriage and relationships, we are confronted with the longings and the selfishness of the human heart, and left up to its own, human nature does not change.

God's nature and character do not change either. He remains the God of love who cared enough for His Creation to redeem it, and He works in people's lives whenever they avail themselves of Him. To make this good news known to the world, He has chosen to partner with the Church and with us individually.

Throughout its history, the Church for the most part has been a vessel of God's grace, although its failings are sometimes newsworthy. It continues to have a crucial role to play in encouraging people to make responsible choices and to accept love, not selfishness, as the better thing to embrace. The Church does this when it preaches the Gospel of God's love towards mankind, makes known the Great Commandments to love God and our neighbor, and acts as a community of loving individuals. In doing these things, the Church draws a critical contrast between unconditional love and selfishness masquerading as love.

On the question of marriage, Thomas Martin advised: "The Christian message should warn people that marriage will not be easy."[3] Such a message, if taken seriously, would encourage people to manage their expectations of marriage accordingly, so that their dream mate does not turn into a nightmare. The Church also does well when it makes clear that marriage is meant to be permanent: "'The man who hates and divorces his wife,' says the LORD, the God of Israel, 'does violence to the one he should protect,' says the LORD Almighty. So be on your guard, and do not be unfaithful." (Malachi 2:16) Moreover, the Church must not shy away from the Biblical understanding that sex, by God's design, is to be reserved for marriage. Such clear declarations will probably not be well received by society at large—and perhaps not even by many parishioners, such is now the state of affairs—but they need to be heard. This is no time for trying to maintain the cultural status quo, if for no other reason than it is not worth maintaining.

The parents of underage children have a unique role to play. Parents—even if they themselves have failed in various ways earlier in life—should not compound that failure by neglecting to teach their children. In particular, they should teach their children what they know of God and of right and wrong. They should put their children first, before their own desire for personal success, by taking an active interest in their children's lives and how their children spend their time. Parents should teach their children the importance of being responsible, especially the importance of delayed gratification, which is so important to many areas of life, including education, career, finances, love, and romance. Husbands and wives should stay married, thereby helping to break the cycle of divorce, and otherwise set the best example they can for their children.

It is only natural to long for a culture that reflects God's best, both out of a desire to live in a better world and out of concern for the lost among us. It is hard not to be discouraged as we survey the cultural landscape, but in a sense we shouldn't be surprised at what we see. This is a fallen world after all, and we are told by Jesus that Satan is the "prince of this world" (John 14:30). The Apostle Paul characterized the role of Christians as being "ambassadors" for Christ on earth (2 Corinthians 5:20). Inherent in this metaphor is the idea that the Christian is to represent a different perspective, a different culture. At its best, then, Christianity is countercultural, since the dominant culture is not God-centered.

While things here on earth are definitely not heavenly, whether a particular culture will get relatively better or worse at any given time is another matter. Just as it is not preordained that someone in a given situation will do the wrong thing, no one can say with certainty whether the culture in any country will decline in the coming decades. After all, each person contributes to the culture, which is the sum total of everyone's individual contribution. Although we are certainly influenced by the behavior of those around us, culture is not something that is imposed on us, as if it were a mysterious force out there or something determined by a committee handing out guidelines—rather, each individual's behavior constitutes one vote, as it were, for what the culture will be. The culture changes when people change. If we don't like the dominant culture of selfishness, we can "vote" with our behavior for a *counterculture* of love of God, love of one's neighbor, and God-pleasing values.

Such a counterculture is sorely needed and—by God's grace—would become the dominant culture, if only most would embrace it. Imagine the difference that would make! A society in which men and women do not treat each other as objects but learn to respect each other as persons. A society in which adults enter into marriage thoughtfully and only after counting the cost. A society in which marriage lasts a lifetime, and adults as well as their children are spared the ravages of divorce. In short, a society in which unconditional love is a way of life.

Even if most would not choose such a culture, it remains everyone's responsibility to do the right thing and to set an example for those who would not. The dominant culture is challenged whenever an individual—regardless of his or her marital status—does the right thing. At that point everyone watching is encouraged to also make right choices. In a real sense, the challenge to all of us is a dare—a dare to be different than what the dominant culture would have us be, a dare to live righteously and build God's Kingdom of love.

ACKNOWLEDGMENTS

I EXTEND MY thanks to many for their thoughtful reviews: Pastor Scott Perry, Marie Russell, and the young adults group, all at Holy Cross Lutheran Church of Los Gatos, California; Malia Formes, PhD, Joerg Opherk, PhD, Cheri Newman, and Pastor Don Follis; and members of the extended Johnson family—Lois, David Christopher, Sarah, and Iris, PhD. Thanks also go to Joleen Graumann, Maria Gagliano, and Jennifer Eck for their editorial reviews and to Pastor Ron Simkins, whose teachings have influenced much of my thinking.

Finally, I gratefully acknowledge here the many publishers and authors who have a generous copyright permissions policy or otherwise responded favorably to my requests to reproduce excerpts from their publications.

Ellen K. Rothman, *Hands and Hearts: A History of Courtship in America* (Cambridge: Harvard University Press, 1987). Courtesy of Ellen K. Rothman.

William Graham Cole, *Sex and Love in the Bible* (New York: Association Press, 1959). Copyright by National Board of Young Men's Christian Associations.

Beth L. Bailey, *From Front Porch to Back Seat: Courtship in Twentieth-Century America*, pp. 15–16, 81, and 141. Copyright © 1988 by Johns Hopkins University Press. Reprinted with permission of Johns Hopkins University Press.

Kathleen A. Bogle, *Hooking Up: Sex, Dating, and Relationships on Campus* (New York: New York University Press, 2008).

Philip Lyndon Reynolds, *Marriage in the Western Church* (Boston: Brill Academic Publishers, 2001).

Paul Hollander, *Extravagant Expectations: New Ways to Find Romantic Love in America* (Chicago: Ivan R. Dee, 2011).

Dorothy C. Holland and Margaret A. Eisenhart, *Educated in Romance: Women, Achievement, and College Culture* (Chicago: University of Chicago Press, 1990).

Wendy Shalit, *A Return to Modesty: Discovering the Lost Virtue* (New York: Free Press, 1999).

Ron Simkins, *Sexuality: A Dimension of God's Glory* (a Bible study of New Covenant Fellowship, Champaign, Illinois, November 1978). Courtesy of Ron Simkins.

Frances and Joseph Gies, *Marriage and the Family in the Middle Ages* (New York: HarperCollins, 1987). Courtesy of HarperCollins Publishers.

Stephanie Coontz, *Marriage, a History* (New York: Penguin Books, 2006).

John Powell, *Unconditional Love.* © 1978, 1999 RCL Benziger, a Kendall Hunt Company, Cincinnati, OH 45249. Used by permission.

Drew Dyck, "The Leavers," *Christianity Today*, November 2010.

Ernest Earnest, *The American Eve in Fact and Fiction, 1775 –1914* (Urbana: University of Illinois Press, 1974).

Dietrich Bonhoeffer, *Letters and Papers from Prison* (Minneapolis: Fortress Press, 2015).

Thomas M. Martin, *The Challenge of Christian Marriage: Marriage in Scripture, History and Contemporary Life* (New York: Paulist Press, 1990).

NOTES

Chapter 1

1 There is admittedly ambiguity surrounding the meaning of the words "date" and "dating." Here a date is taken to be a prearranged social meeting between two persons of different genders that is characterized at least in part by romantic undertones. Dating is taken to mean a series of such meetings, in which romance plays an important role.

2 For related ideas, see Kathleen A. Bogle, *Hooking Up: Sex, Dating, and Relationships on Campus* (New York: New York University Press, 2008), p. 206.

3 As the reference to royal pursuits makes clear, this notion of social rankings goes back a long time. In 1937, Willard Waller made a similar observation in studying dating on the college campus and characterized the interaction between men and women as one of "rating and dating" ("The Rating and Dating Complex," *American Sociological Review*, vol. 2, 1937, pp. 727–734). I have chosen the metaphor "social totem pole," which emphasizes the notion of perceived superiority and inferiority.

4 Dorothy C. Holland and Margaret A. Eisenhart, *Educated in Romance: Women, Achievement, and College Culture* (Chicago: University of Chicago Press, 1990; paperback 1992), p. 99.

5 Ibid., p. 8.

6 Willard Waller observed in the 1930s that an unbalanced gender ratio within a group gave the gender in the minority increased "bargaining power" (Waller, "The Rating and Dating Complex," p. 732).

7   Henry David Thoreau, *Walden*, 1854.

8   Samuel Johnson's description of a second marriage, as quoted by James Boswell, *The Life of Samuel Johnson, LL.D.*, 1791.

Chapter 2

1   Blaise Pascal, *The Thoughts of Blaise Pascal* (London: George Bell and Sons, 1901), p. 95. (Original work published 1670.) This translation is consistent with more recent ones, which generally appear under the title *Pensées*.

2   John Powell, *Unconditional Love* (Cincinnati: RCL Benziger, 1999), p. 70.

3   Alan Loy McGinnis discusses factors such as these in his book *The Friendship Factor: How to Get Closer to the People You Care For* (Minneapolis: Augsburg Books, 2004).

4   Pastor Ron Simkins of the New Covenant Fellowship in Champaign, Illinois, observed that "use and discard" is the underlying philosophy of many relationships. Further thoughts of his on this subject appear in chapter 7.

Chapter 4

1   Edward Westermarck, *The History of Human Marriage* (London: Macmillan, 1901); Stephanie Coontz, *Marriage, a History* (New York: Penguin Books, 2006).

2   Frances and Joseph Gies, *Marriage and the Family in the Middle Ages* (New York: HarperCollins, 1987; paperback 1989).

3   Westermarck, *The History of Human Marriage*; William Graham Cole, *Sex and Love in the Bible* (New York: Association Press, 1959).

4   Cole, *Sex and Love in the Bible*, p. 239.

5   Philip Lyndon Reynolds, *Marriage in the Western Church* (Boston: Brill Academic Publishers, 2001), p. 11.

6   Reynolds, *Marriage in the Western Church*.

7   Ibid., p. 22.

8   Reynolds, *Marriage in the Western Church*; Westermarck, *The History of Human Marriage*; Gies and Gies, *Marriage and the Family in the Middle Ages*; Thomas M. Martin, *The Challenge of Christian Marriage: Marriage*

in Scripture, History and Contemporary Life (New York: Paulist Press, 1990).

9   Reynolds, *Marriage in the Western Church*; Gies and Gies, *Marriage and the Family in the Middle Ages.*

10 Martin, *The Challenge of Christian Marriage*; Reynolds, *Marriage in the Western Church*; Cole, *Sex and Love in the Bible*; Westermarck, *The History of Human Marriage.*

11 Reynolds, *Marriage in the Western Church*, p. 316.

12 Martin, *The Challenge of Christian Marriage*; Reynolds, *Marriage in the Western Church.*

13 Reynolds, *Marriage in the Western Church*, p. 75.

14 Gies and Gies, *Marriage and the Family in the Middle Ages*; Coontz, *Marriage, a History.*

15 Gies and Gies, *Marriage and the Family in the Middle Ages*, p. 117.

16 Gies and Gies, *Marriage and the Family in the Middle Ages*; Martin, *The Challenge of Christian Marriage*; Coontz, *Marriage, a History.*

17 Gies and Gies, *Marriage and the Family in the Middle Ages*, p. 297.

18 Coontz, *Marriage, a History*; Gies and Gies, *Marriage and the Family in the Middle Ages.* As noted by Coontz and Gies and Gies, among the well-to-do, an individual's desires and preferences actually played less of a role in selecting a marriage partner than it did among those in the peasant class. An upper-class marriage might be arranged, keeping in mind both the personal attributes of a spouse as well as the opportunity to forge an alliance between families. Those in the noble class commonly negotiated marriages, with kings and queens looking for ways to forge alliances between countries.

19 Coontz, *Marriage, a History*; Martin, *The Challenge of Christian Marriage*; Gies and Gies, *Marriage and the Family in the Middle Ages.*

20 Gies and Gies, *Marriage and the Family in the Middle Ages*; Coontz, *Marriage, a History.*

21 Coontz, *Marriage, a History.*

22 Ibid., p. 5.

Chapter 5

1   Ellen K. Rothman, *Hands and Hearts: A History of Courtship in America* (Cambridge: Harvard University Press, 1987). By examining letters and other writings from Colonial times through the early 1900s, Rothman reconstructed attitudes that were prevalent during earlier eras, at least among white, native-born, middle- and upper-class Protestant Americans, who did most of the contemporaneous writing and are thus responsible for most of the available source material. Of course, life was different if you were poor, an immigrant, black, and/or a slave.

2   Ibid., p. 23. The nested quote has been rewritten to exactly match the original quotation, which was taken from Ernest Earnest, *The American Eve in Fact and Fiction, 1775–1914* (Urbana: University of Illinois Press, 1974), p. 72.

3   Rothman, *Hands and Hearts*.

4   Ibid., p. 36–37. Rothman found that the meaning of the word "friend" has evolved. During Colonial times, it was commonly used in reference to relatives; in the late 1700s, it came to be applied to non-relatives, with the terms "friendship" and "love" being complementary in some sense. During the 1800s, however, the meaning of those terms became decoupled from each other (see main text).

5   Ibid., p. 37.

6   Ibid., pp. 39–40, 103.

7   Ibid., p. 101.

8   Rothman, *Hands and Hearts*; Karen Lystra, *Searching the Heart: Women, Men, and Romantic Love in Nineteenth-Century America* (New York: Oxford University Press, 1989; paperback, 1992).

9   "At Home with the Editor," *Ladies' Home Journal*, April 1892, p. 12.

10   Rothman, *Hands and Hearts*, p. 176.

11   Rothman, *Hands and Hearts*; Lystra, *Searching the Heart*.

12   Rothman, *Hands and Hearts*, p. 109.

13   Lystra, *Searching the Heart*. Lystra discerned the attitudes of Americans towards romance from the letters of more than one

hundred persons whose demographics were similar to those of Rothman, *Hands and Hearts.*

14 Lystra, *Searching the Heart,* pp. 29, 186.

15 Lystra, *Searching the Heart;* Rothman, *Hands and Hearts.*

16 Lystra, *Searching the Heart.*

17 Ibid., pp. 11, 20.

18 Lystra, *Searching the Heart.*

19 Ibid.

20 Beth L. Bailey, *From Front Porch to Back Seat: Courtship in Twentieth-Century America* (Baltimore: Johns Hopkins University Press, 1988; paperback, 1989), pp. 15–16.

21 Ibid., p. 16.

22 Bailey, *From Front Porch to Back Seat;* Rothman, *Hands and Hearts.*

23 Bailey, *From Front Porch to Back Seat,* p. 81.

24 Rothman, *Hands and Hearts,* p. 225.

25 Bailey, *From Front Porch to Back Seat;* Rothman, *Hands and Hearts.*

26 Bailey, *From Front Porch to Back Seat,* p. 141.

27 Bailey, *From Front Porch to Back Seat;* Rothman, *Hands and Hearts;* Lystra, *Searching the Heart.*

28 Bogle, *Hooking Up.*

29 Ibid., pp. 47–48.

30 Ibid., p. 57.

31 Ibid., chapter 7.

32 Paul Hollander, *Extravagant Expectations: New Ways to Find Romantic Love in America* (Chicago: Ivan R. Dee, 2011), pp. 104–105.

33 Ibid., p. 132.

34 Jean M. Twenge, "Have Smartphones Destroyed a Generation?" *The Atlantic,* September 2017.

35 Reynolds, *Marriage in the Western Church,* pp. 252–254.

Chapter 6

1   Martin, *The Challenge of Christian Marriage*, p. 131.

2   Benjamin Franklin, *Poor Richard's Almanack*, 1738.

3   Wendy Shalit, *A Return to Modesty: Discovering the Lost Virtue* (New York: Free Press, 1999), pp. 121, 172.

4   Similar ideas are discussed by John Powell in *Why Am I Afraid to Tell You Who I Am?* (Cincinnati: RCL Benziger, 1998).

5   Joshua Harris aptly described lust, infatuation, and self-pity as "pollutants" of the heart in his book *I Kissed Dating Goodbye* (Sisters, Oregon: Multnomah Books, 1997).

6   Hollander, *Extravagant Expectations*, p. 198.

Chapter 7

1   Drew Dyck, "The Leavers," *Christianity Today*, November 2010, p. 42.

2   Cole, *Sex and Love in the Bible*, pp. 425–426.

3   Ibid., p. 341.

4   Ron Simkins, *Sexuality: A Dimension of God's Glory* (a Bible study of New Covenant Fellowship, Champaign, Illinois, November 1978).

5   Billy Graham, *Just as I Am: The Autobiography of Billy Graham* (New York: HarperCollins, 1997).

6   Bogle, *Hooking Up*, p. 85.

7   Ibid., p. 89–90.

Afterword

1   Dietrich Bonhoeffer, *Letters and Papers from Prison* (Minneapolis: Fortress Press, 2015), p.18. (Original work written 1942.)

2   See, for example, chapters 15–17 of Coontz, *Marriage, a History*, for a discussion of how the expectations surrounding marriage have changed in the United States over the last several decades.

3   Martin, *The Challenge of Christian Marriage*, p. 132.

ABOUT THE AUTHOR

DANIEL E. JOHNSON studied math and physics at the University of Virginia and earned a PhD in physics from the University of Illinois. (You can call him "Doctor" after he performs his first operation; until then, it's "Dan.") After that he served as an officer in the US Air Force and worked as a post-doctoral researcher at the University of Würzburg in Germany. He currently works in the legal field in Silicon Valley (California), where he is the happy husband of one wife and the proud father of their son.

He is a scientist by profession and a philosopher at heart, a Christian who believes in an ordered universe. For him, faith and reason are complementary, not contradictory. He believes they allow us to think about things from different perspectives, to explore the world of ideas, and to arrive at deeper understanding, thereby impacting the culture.

One topic at the intersection of faith, reason, and culture that has always fascinated him is how men and women treat each other. The subject of this book—his first—is something he has been thinking about almost his entire life, although most of its content grew out of his thoughts and experiences as a young adult, prior to getting married. He has been able to test those ideas over time, arriving at a presentation that he hopes is insightful, helpful to the reader, and true to Christian values.

Visit him online at www.dangoodbooks.com or leave a book review at www.amazon.com.

34032221R00110

Made in the USA
San Bernardino, CA
30 April 2019